"Hal Milton brings to bear on the questions of this book his 25 years as a student of the profound ways we embody our personal histories in voice, gesture and movement, combined with his long involvement as a teacher of performance. From the viewpoint of his profound knowledge of these areas, he gives concrete and lively suggestions on how to enter the public world with an authenticity liberated from old fears and self-consciousness. I have always found Hal's work sensitive and helpful."

Don Hanlon
author of *Bone, Breath and Gesture: Practices of Embodiment*
and director of the Somatics Graduate Degree Program at
The California Institute of Integral Studies in San Francisco

"*Going Public* is invaluable for those of us who have dreaded the thought of stepping into the spotlight and find it difficult to maintain our center once we are there. It is a totally unique approach to develop and integrate our grace and wholeness on the outside as well as the inside. I found *Going Public* to be life changing. It will positively affect the reader in countless aspects of bringing forward their true selves."

Dr. Benjamin Shield
author of *Handbook for the Soul, Healers on Healing* and
For the Love of God

"*Going Public* is real. From the first glimpse of the author pressing past his own fears of singing in public to the many ways we can set ourselves free, Hal Milton is there with us, holding our hand. His success stories assure us that no matter what specific issues we have with standing out and being noticed, other people with the same issues already used Hal's skills to get into the limelight."

Susan Collins
author of *Our Children Are Watching: Ten Skills for Leading
the Next Generation to Success*

"For 23 years Hal Milton has impressed and inspired me with the consistency of his search for personal essence and for effective healing techniques. *Going Public* documents the transformative and spiritual power of the work he employs. In this book you will learn how to free the body, mind, emotions and spirit, and realize your true self in any situation."

Carlos Warter, Ph.D., M.D.
author of *Recovery of the Sacred*

"*Going Public* is an excellent guide to claiming and authentically expressing your personal power. This book tells you how to become friends with your body, your mind and your Spirit so that you can truly become a Star!"

Robert Brumet
Unity minister, educator and author of *Finding Yourself in Transition*

"Rewarding and exciting! Milton skillfully helps us all 'Go Public' and find our inner star."

David and Gay Lynn Williamson
authors of *Transformative Rituals: Celebrations for Personal Growth*

Your authentic expression is a blessing to all you touch

Hal Milton

GOING PUBLIC

GOING PUBLIC

A Practical Guide to Developing Personal Charisma

HAL MILTON

Health Communications, Inc.
Deerfield Beach, Florida

Library of Congress Catalog-in-Publication Data

Milton, Hal, date
  Going public: a practical guide to developing personal charisma /
Hal Milton.
    p. cm.
  Includes bibliographical references.
  ISBN 1-55874-360-X (pbk.)
  1. Public speaking. 2. Acting. 3. Rolfing. I. Title.
PN4121.M5625 1995   95-35399
808.5--dc20   CIP

Publisher: Health Communications, Inc.
            3201 S.W. 15th Street
            Deerfield Beach, Florida 33442-8190

Cover design by Linda Golden

I dedicate this book to my parents, Sam and Pauline; my wife, Sonya; and to my adult children, Kenyon, Tamara and Kameron, for all they have taught and continue to teach me. *Shalom aleichem.*

CONTENTS

FOREWORD

I suspect that much of the good that Hal has done with (STAR) Success Through Active Response has been derived from the other things that he has done for himself—thinking neither of performance nor profession. Even without having been a witness to his workshop, I am sure that what he brings to bear on the task of assisting others toward being themselves in public performance situations is the result of his own overall psycho-spiritual ripening.

It is appropriate that I say this because it fell on me to be Pied Piper to him over 20 years ago, when—on returning from my Arica Pilgrimage—I was invited (along with Adnan el-Sarhan) to teach an Orange County, California group of which he was part. That was before the Seekers After Truth (SAT) Institute crystallized in Berkeley, and Hal then became one of the participants in that pioneering semi-secret adventure in which it was emphasized that this would not be a training of any kind and that all learning should be regarded as something for "internal use" only. In the course of it I came to appreciate his courage as he learned to be himself and express his true feelings, and so it is no great surprise that he has been helping others do the same. This, of course, he does in a way that reflects the personal mosaic of the various skills and trainings acquired along his life—from Rolfing to Unity Ministry.

Other than celebrating Hal Milton as a good and able person, I would like to celebrate his subject, which pleases me very much. For I think singing is not only worth writing about, but celebrating in song. Because I believe that musical enjoyment is spiritual nourishment in disguise, I think it is not trivial to hope that this book furthers the joy of singing.

Claudio Naranjo

ACKNOWLEDGMENTS

Great appreciation is due to . . .

My many students, clients and participants in Rolfing®[1], Movement Education and the STAR Performance workshops. You have truly been my teachers.

Those wonderful volunteers who worked tirelessly to serve: Brian and Nancy Farnsworth Coleman, Susanna Gray, Charles Lane, Carolyn Ringo Levins, Debra Blevins, Lisa Rogness, Pam and David Merrill, Dianne Ross and the other wonderful unnamed people who helped.

My partners and collaborators in the early formation of STAR: Anny Eastwood and Toni Land.

John Daniel for his initial guidance and support.

Lynda Rae for the tireless hours of creative writing and editing. Catherine Moirai, who conscientiously reworked the manuscript into its final form.

The staff at Health Communications, Inc., who have been warm, friendly and helpful, particularly

---

1. Rolfing is a service mark of the Rolf Institute of Structural Integration.

Christine Belleris, Kathryn Butterfield, Matthew Diener, Marsha Donohoe, Jan Werblin, Gary Seidler, Peter Vegso and Kim Weiss.

Lance Livesay, who captured the essence of my words and created marvelous illustrations. My first mentor, Dr. Lawrence Mathae, who has no idea how his wisdom has influenced my path.

I am grateful for the teachers who guided me through Zen, Vippassana, Tibetan Dzogchen, Sufism, Christianity (Unity), Hinduism and Judaism; all the teachers who taught, nurtured and encouraged me to continue the work they transmitted, namely Dr. Ida Rolf, Judith Aston, Dr. Claudio Naranjo, Bob Hoffman (Quadrinity Process), Dr. Ernest Pecci, Harry Martin and J.R.; the teachers, staff and colleagues of The Rolf Institute, the Guild for Structural Integration, Unity School, and the Association of Unity Churches; Unity of Knoxville for an opportunity to teach and learn; the Reverend Jim Peterson for his vision and support; the Reverend Stretton Smith for his 4T program; Wayne Levine for his legal assistance; and especially my wife, Sonya, who supported, edited and encouraged the sharing of my credo through this book.

Names and identifying features of clients described in this book have been changed to protect their privacy. However, all stories are true. I am indebted to them for their willingness to risk and share.

INTRODUCTION

Twenty-four years ago when I was studying to become a therapist, I attended a month-long training program at the Gestalt Institute of Los Angeles. During the second week of the training one of the instructors announced that there would be an optional evening session in which a new form of body work call "Rolfing" would be demonstrated to the group. He asked for a volunteer who was willing to be "Rolfed"—someone who was willing to be the demonstration model for the coming evening session. For some unexplainable reason I raised my hand.

That evening I found myself lying on my back on a mat on the floor, clad in only my underwear, while 50 other participants huddled around to watch a man I had never met before work on releasing the deep muscular tension in the upper half of my body.

Slowly, gently and with expert skill, this "Rolfer" worked on the muscles of my chest and stomach releasing patterns of tension that had been built up and maintained over twenty six years of repressed and constricted living that included eighteen years growing up in a dysfunctional home, seven years in a military school and four years at an Ivy League college.

For the first half hour this gentle but powerful man worked on the left side of my chest. When he was finished, he asked me to observe my chest as I breathed. Each time I inhaled, the left side of my rib cage rose almost a full inch higher than the right side. It was truly amazing! I had no idea how locked up my body had become. And as a result, both my sense of aliveness and my self-expression had become severely constricted as well. By the end of the evening I felt more alive, more open and more at peace with myself than I had in years.

This gentle, loving man with the magic hands who had begun the process of releasing my body and my spirit was Hal Milton. When I thanked him for what he had done for me, Hal just smiled that gentle radiant smile of his and said, "That's all right. Just keep sharing who you truly are with people. That is all the repayment I need." Because of the personal transformation I experienced, which began through my work with Hal that night, my life has become a series of miracles. I went on the become an internationally known speaker, seminar leader and trainer. I am known for how calm, relaxed, loving and joyful I am as I speak and lead groups. I now feel at home in my body and in front of cameras or large audiences.

I have appeared on hundreds of television and radio shows including *20/20, Eye to Eye* and the *Tom Snyder Show*. I have recorded twelve successful audio and video training programs and spoken with comfort and ease to over 500,000 people, including an audience of 12,000 dentists at their national conference. I have played the guitar and sung as part of my

presentations, and I have even created a short stand up com-
edy act that I sometimes use in my workshops.

That first night that Hal worked on me was the last I saw of
Hal for almost seven years. I returned to the east cost where I
finished ten more sessions of Rolfing with another practition-
er, and Hal continued his practice in body work in California.

Unknown to me, Hal was developing and teaching his
S.T.A.R. Performance Training. Seven years later, when I
returned to Los Angeles to join the staff of a Santa Monica
based training company, Hal was conducting his S.T.A.R.
Performance Trainings in the same building in which we
conducted our trainings.

One weekend, a student from Hal's training session asked
me to attend the graduation evening of his workshop. Since
I also knew some of the other participants, I decided to
attend. I was blown away! People who I had known for over a
year as shy and reticent were belting out difficult songs in
front of over a hundred strangers. Using the same powerful
techniques he teaches in this book, Hal had magically
released not only their natural talent but their charisma,
humor and unique charm in only a few short days. I was truly
impressed with his magical ability to help so many people
release their true selves in front of others in such a short
period of time.

Most of these people did not attend the training to
become professional singers. And yet, by eliciting their fears
of performing in front of an audience and helping them to
overcome them, Hal had assisted these people in confronting
and mastering all the other fears that might be blocking their
self-expression. Their self-esteem and self-confidence had

quantum leaped in the space of a weekend workshop. The effects translated into every area of their lives and lasted as long as I knew these people.

In this remarkably simple and yet powerful book, Hal shares these same simple yet powerful principles and techniques with you. You can learn to overcome your fears, connect with your natural genius and show up with charisma, humor and presence in a way that you never dreamed possible before. I encourage you to use this book to take yourself into a larger public arena—whatever that may be for you. You will find that, as a result, you will enjoy yourself more, create bigger results in your life and make more of a difference in the lives of others.

I believe that we are at a time in our history when the world needs each of us to be all we can be and do all we can do to contribute to the needs of the whole. We cannot do that when we are locked up by our irrational fears, controlled by our limiting beliefs and trapped inside a non-responsive body. This book can teach anyone how to connect with and express their highest purpose.

Nothing is more rewarding to ourselves or contributes more to others than increasing our levels of self-awareness and self-expression. Hal Milton gave us all a great gift when he took the time to capture the essence of his work in a way that we can all access and use.

I wish you the best experience possible as you read this book and put its techniques to work in your life! Expect many miracles to occur as a result!

Jack Canfield
Co-author *of Chicken Soup for the Soul*

RISKY BUSINESS:
THE BIRTH OF A STAR

I sat at the back of the auditorium, my eyes riveted to an empty stage. The house lights were dimmed and the stage was lit by soft footlights. The video cameras were rolling; the pianist was rearranging her sheet music; the audience was shuffling in restless anticipation. In a few moments I would watch the first soloist of the evening step into the spotlight. I waited with a mixture of pride, exhilaration and empathy, knowing this performance marked a milestone in the lives of 20 people who had walked into my weekend workshop several days ago—scared, uncertain, expectant and willing to cross the comfort barrier that had prevented them from experiencing the hidden "star" within each of them. This was the graduation concert for STAR Performance (Success Through Active Response)—a workshop that uses the medium of solo vocal performance as a means to help people learn how to risk, how to communicate authentically, and how to realize the star potential within themselves.

Why singing? There are very few singers in our society. If the truth be known, there are probably a good many singers-in-the-shower and just as many freeway singers crooning along to their car radios on the way to work. But very few people sing publicly in modern life, and only a few actually perform in front of people. Try this. Ask somebody, on the spur of the moment, to stand up before a room full of people and sing a song. You'll get a standard response almost every time: "I can't sing," or "I'm not in good voice tonight," or "I always forget the words," or "Sing? Me?" The response isn't surprising. Solo singing may be one of the most frightening risks a person can take.

A survey of commonly held fears ranked public speaking as number one—higher than sickness, poverty, snakes, being buried alive or even death. According to *The Book of Lists*, people fear public speaking (#1) more than death (#7)[1]: most people would rather die than stand up and speak in front of an audience. Although public singing wasn't on that list, I am convinced, through my personal experience as well as what I've learned from observing people in my workshops, that solo singing before an audience carries even more trauma than public speaking. The

---

1. David Wallenchinsky, Irving Wallace and Amy Wallace, *The Book of Lists* (New York: William Morrow & Co., 1977), 469.

mere idea of singing a song alone in front of others terrifies most people. They will agree that anyone who will sing solo in public can do anything else life asks of them.

What makes public singing so traumatic in our culture? We live in an age overloaded with mass media. Gone are the days when families gathered around the piano each evening after supper to sing the latest popular music. Now we let a sound system or TV sing for us, and people who sing in public must be slick professionals or those hoping to break into show business. Even those rare individuals who don't experience terror at the thought of public singing often get trapped in their image of how it ought to be done. They mimic the gestures, tone and style of someone they have seen, and the performance becomes pseudo-Sinatra or would-be-Whitney. The particular mystique of solo singing—the cultural custom that performing belongs only to a chosen few—makes it the ideal tool for teaching the skill that so many people in today's society seem to need: risk-taking.

In my personal experience, singing was indeed risky business. No one was ever told more often than I as a boy, "Hal, just mouth the words." At some point in childhood I accepted as fact that I could not carry a tune. I had no sense of rhythm. I always forgot the words. I sang flat. In short, I was not musical. I wasn't happy with my "deficiency," but I lived with it for 40 years.

Eventually, though, I experienced an irresistible urge to learn to play the guitar—a foolish urge for one who has studiously avoided making music all his life. The urge came upon me as I was visiting a friend in Berkeley,

Michael Lorimer, a classical guitarist and protégé of Andrés Segovia. I was enamored with his music, and one night I gained enough courage to confess to him my deepest desire and dread.

"Music was a real black hole in my life," I explained. "We never even had a record player in my family. Music simply had no value to my parents and they always discouraged me from learning to play an instrument. They told me that if I started music lessons I would probably just quit. I managed to fulfill their prophecy: Every time I tried to learn anything related to music, I failed. Everyone concluded that I was tone deaf. So here I am, four decades later, wanting to see if I can conquer my failure at music. What should I do?"

He laughed. "It's simple," he said. "Just do it."

It wasn't that simple. I managed to learn to play a few chords, but my guitar teacher told me, once again, that I was tone deaf. I went from teacher to teacher with no results. Finally my guitar teacher told me of Eddie Ruhl, a famous opera singer who was taking a six-month vacation in my hometown of Santa Barbara, California. I learned that he was accepting a few students and begged my guitar teacher to arrange an audition. Eddie was a portly man with an enormous chest and a powerful voice. Surprisingly, he said I was *not* tone deaf. In fact, he insisted that I had a good voice and just needed some training. During the next six months, he took me under his wing. For the first time in my life, the pre-conceived negative ideas about my singing ability began to crumble. Suddenly I was belting out classical Italian music in a strong bass voice.

Soon he left town, but I was hooked. I started taking performance classes. Still, I would sing off-key in the middle of a song and I remember one of my performance teachers asking me, "Why do you want to do this to yourself, sing in public?" I told him that I didn't care how I sounded, I just wanted to conquer my fear.

My first performance was in a small local coffee house, and I invited two of my teenage children to come and listen. They had not wanted to come, and as I blundered through my song, off-key, I watched them out of the corner of my eye: Their feet shuffled; their eyes were lowered; and I saw how embarrassed they were for me. I stopped in the middle of my song. My fingers felt wooden and my voice had gone dry. I looked at the audience. They were quietly waiting to hear what I had to give them: I gave them my nervousness; I gave them my song; and in the process, I gave them myself. In turn, they gave me an ovation and I haven't been the same since. I had no illusions about my musical skill at that point, nor do I now, but I also had no doubt that I'd communicated authentically with my audience, and it was an electric moment for all of us.

In my own life, voice training and public performance became a vehicle to outwit myself, to free myself from the inner voices that held me back from exploring music— that held me back from so many other rich, daring experiences in my life.

I soon discovered how many other people listened to these same inner voices. "I can't carry a tune," they would tell me when asked to sing.

"But you're among friends here."

"All the worse," they would mumble. "Who wants your friends to hear what a wimpy voice you have?"

"Nobody's judging you."

"I'm judging myself!"

That was true. I could hear the judgmental voices echoing in the caverns of their minds—mothers, fathers, older brothers, teachers, childhood friends, high school sweethearts—all of them laughing up their sleeves at this squeaky, flat voice. How do you answer a fear born of a lifetime of judgments?

You answer: "Do it anyway!"

This same answer applies equally to those people with good voices, even trained voices, who, in spite of their talent, suffer from stage fright or a fear of being judged. Solo vocal performance seems to bring up all the issues and considerations born of a lifetime of listening to other people's voices and trying to become what we thought they wanted us to be. In fact, we can fall victim to the same sorts of negative considerations every day, not just in singing, but in the countless routine acts of ordinary bravery that make up the performance of our lives—asking for a date, signing a contract, meeting a client, asking for seconds, saying yes, saying no. If we gave in to these considerations every time, we'd never attempt anything new. Fortunately, most of us are not so severely blocked as to be immobile. But many of us allow our considerations to limit us in a variety of ways—procrastinating, staying stuck in unsatisfactory jobs or relationships, yearning for something more. We long to say what is in our hearts, to live out loud, to go public with our feelings and our desires. And the only answer that will move us from considerations to success is: "Do it anyway."

Fear is the number one emotion that limits success in all areas of life. Risking is the way out. The willingness to take a chance sets you free. Perhaps the most fundamental place to begin is with your body. Your physical body is a tool that can be used to assist you in becoming free to move beyond the fears and limitations that have shaped your life. As a student of the physiology of exercise and an athletic coach, I saw fears and considerations reflected in the ways people moved and held their bodies. In my professional experience with Rolfing® (a system of soft-tissue reorganization to balance and align the body)[2] and as a counselor in movement education, I was trained to notice stress, disharmony and tension in the carriage of the body. Stress and tension in the body parallel and reflect stress and tension in the mind and emotions. Our body configurations are living pictures of our histories, coats of armor developed through years of physical and emotional tension. This tension creates uncomfortable holding patterns in the body, inappropriate adjustments to the field of gravity. These holding patterns affect how we sit, stand, walk and even breathe. They may be the result of early childhood training, those voices that said, "Stand up straight," "Be tall," or "Hold your stomach in," or they may be the result of specific emotional traumas. Physical holding patterns certainly affect how we communicate

---

2. Rolfing is a service mark of the Rolf Institute of Structural Integration.

with others. If we are not relaxed and at home in our own bodies, we have a hard time relating to other people authentically.

Clearly one way to confront fear and limitation, then, is to act directly upon the body. Using Rolfing and movement education, we can clear out some of the hesitations built into our physiology. We can learn to feel and act at home in the field of gravity, rather than fight it. Our bodies can become more flexible and resilient, our motions more fluid and responsive. The result of this physical reeducation is life-changing, dramatic and gratifying. As tension is eased out and the body's intrinsic harmony takes over, a corresponding change happens in the emotional state.

Through my experience as a Rolfer, I discovered that as I unwrapped the physical armoring in my clients' bodies, an essential beauty emerged—an essence that I have come to call "star quality." This star quality emerged by restructuring the shape of their bodies, thereby restructuring the shape of their world, their perceptions and feelings. As my clients let go of physical constrictions, there was literally more physical space in their bodies and they started feeling lighter. As movement patterns changed and they started feeling more grounded, with their feet solidly balanced on the floor, they also experienced more emotional security. As their bodies began working more efficiently without the limiting restrictions of years of conditioned binding, this greater *physical* ease cleared the way for greater *emotional* ease and better communication with family, lovers, business colleagues, intimate friends, casual friends and strangers. I watched people's lives change and stars emerge.

As I witnessed the intimate partnership between the body, mind and emotions, I began to realize the necessity for an experiential process that would challenge and stimulate people to move past their limitations physically, mentally and emotionally. I wanted to create an environment that would uncover that star quality and allow it to emerge free and undaunted. I realized that what holds us back and keeps us from being the stars we could be is a constellation of cautions, fears and negative considerations; a complex cycle of physical, mental and emotional limitations. I decided that breaking out of the morass would simply require taking some risks. Performance— solo singing in front of an audience with microphone and accompanist—is an experience loaded with risk and seemed the perfect medium for the job. Thus, STAR Performance was born.

As coach and facilitator for STAR Performance workshops, I guide people through a set of experiences that is at once challenging and safe, risky yet nonthreatening. Participants learn how to stretch their limits. Once they develop the courage to take a few chances within the context of a comfortable environment, they can apply that courage to important situations in "the real world." I've seen people transformed, in the course of a weekend, from demure to powerful, simply by overcoming their deeply rooted terror of singing alone in front of an audience. And indeed, STAR Performance is not about singing, but about personal power.

According to legend, Cole Porter gave Ethel Merman some valuable advice early in her career. "Ethel," he said, "*never* take singing lessons." Porter was not opposed to voice lessons *per se*, of course. But he recognized that the STAR potential in Ethel Merman depended not on classical training, but on her stage presence, her charisma, her personal power. To this day, Broadway fans argue about Ethel Merman's singing talent, just as they debate her looks and her acting ability; but nobody questions that Merman was a star—one of the greatest stars the Broadway musical stage has ever produced—with a sure-fire ability to sell a song, enchant an audience, bring the house down and create a smash hit.

The first "singing lesson" we give to participants in the workshop is that STAR Performance is not about how well you can sing. We are not in the business of teaching vocal techniques or the theory of music, and I am not a voice coach. There are, of course, countless qualified coaches and schools that teach the theory and mechanics of singing, but we're not concerned with that component of the art. I contend that the greater part of effective performance is not the music—not technique and theory—but the less tangible components of authenticity, confidence and personal power. The real goal of STAR Performance, then, is not to make singers of people (we leave that to the maestros and the music academies), but rather, using singing as a tool, to teach people to risk being authentic. When people see that the greater part of performance depends not on technique but on authentic communication, they automatically bid good-bye to their considerations, excuses and defenses concerning their musical talent or training. At that point they are ready to participate and reap the benefits, for what is left is raw star potential. By dismissing their artificial considerations when solo-singing, they learn that they'll be able to use the personal resources they've gained to be more authentic, effective and convincing with their business associates, lovers, friends and strangers throughout their countless daily performances.

The STAR workshop culminates in a public performance. All weekend we work hard with each participant, individually and within a group, to strip away their considerations, encourage risk-taking and help them be comfortable about sharing themselves. By the end of the weekend, participants sing their songs differently than they anticipated. They are more alive, more honest and, as a result, more communicative. They are stars of their Sunday night performance. Moreover, each new star receives what he or she rightfully deserves: long, loud, heartfelt applause. One of the greatest challenges facing workshop participants may be the final risk of accepting positive attention and believing in it. I have never failed to witness the true star in each performer emerge during this final concert. How long this star quality lasts, and how well it translates to other aspects of their lives outside of the safety of the workshop, depends on how willing they are to continue the risk-taking that they have learned.

This book is a manual for would-be stars. It's a handy map and compass guide through the maze of fears and considerations that keep your essential star quality under wraps. Like life, it is designed to be a participatory experience. Exercises and action steps appear at the end of appropriate chapters to help you translate theory into experience. It's a book about risk-taking—not foolhardy gambling, but rather a more fundamental, more difficult and, in the end, more rewarding act of daring. The risk I advocate is the risk of being authentic and honest, being present and being yourself.

Why is being authentic such a risk? That question is difficult to answer, but I'm certain it's related to why people work so hard (and so painfully) to carry their bodies in a fashion that defies gravity. It also has a lot to do with why people find singing in public so terrifying. We're afraid of being less than perfect, not recognizing that what we have is all there is. We are worthy of value, respect and love just as we are right now.

Risk being yourself; it's all you can really be, anyway. Be present and be honest when dealing with colleagues, with family, with intimates and with strangers. The authenticity of your "performance" will pay off. Clients will remember you if they get the feeling that they really know you. Those dreaded phone calls will be a breeze if all you have to remember is how you really feel and what you really think. And most important, you will have a far greater reward if the love you receive from your friends and lovers is directed to you and not to an imaginary character you've worked so hard to create.

This book is dedicated to the star within you. You were born to shine. It's worth the risk.

"'TIL DEATH DO US PART": MARRYING YOUR BODY, A LIFELONG PARTNERSHIP

Soul and Body, I suggest, react sympathetically upon each other. A change in the state of the soul produces a change in the shape of the body; conversely, a change in the shape of the body produces a change in the state of the soul.

—ARISTOTLE

Life is full of partnerships—marriage partners, business partners, traveling partners, tennis partners. These partners may come and go, but there is one partner who will never desert you until you breathe your last breath—your body. You are wedded to this marvelous creation of bone, muscle, nerve and blood. And since you can't file for divorce, it's a good idea to make sure this marriage is a harmonious one.

The physical body is a mini-universe. Each part of the body—bone, muscle, organs and other soft tissues—has a separate function to perform. Each part of the body needs its own nourishment to function at its optimum potential. However, the individual parts of the body do not function in isolation. Each part is functionally dependent upon the other parts of the body. If each part of the body cooperates with its interdependent parts, then there is smooth and efficient functioning. If, on the other hand, one part of the body is on hold while another is working, this creates greater stress on other areas of the body. Imagine someone raking leaves, digging a ditch, pounding a nail or washing dishes. If much of the body is on hold while the arm is doing all the action—swinging the hammer or washing the dish—then the movement is done at the expense of other parts of the body. Most people work twice as hard as they need to by not allowing their movement to be distributed throughout the body. It is not surprising that people complain about their aching neck or shoulder by day's end.

Ideally, the whole body should respond in varying degrees to each movement, no matter how slight. When there is 100 percent participation in each movement, then the body is truly in partnership with itself, and that ease and efficiency is communicated in its performance. If you look at a champion athlete in action, you will see a partnership of all parts of the body working in harmony with each other, creating a smooth, seemingly effortless performance.

Physical excellence was the focal point of much of my life. As a child I devoured books on anatomy and physiology. As I grew older, nutrition and exercise captured my attention. As a high school, college and Navy athlete, I continually experimented with new ways to keep my body finely tuned. In 1959, with a Master of Science in physical education specializing in the physiology of exercise, I launched my career coaching athletes.

A decade later, I met a spry, 72-year-old woman who turned my entire background in physical education inside out. Her name was Ida P. Rolf. In the late 1960s Gestalt therapist Fritz Perls brought Dr. Rolf to the Esalen Institute in California. As I listened to her describe Rolfing— a technique of body therapy designed to integrate the body's many parts, allowing them to function together harmoniously—my mind reeled. My entire background in physical education had focused on strength building and muscle building, which resulted in contracted, shortened muscles. Now here was this woman who was saying that bodies are supposed to be responsive and resilient, that muscles should be sinewy and lengthened.

Ida Rolf changed my life. Suddenly I had a whole new physical vocabulary, a new criterion for optimum physical fitness. Convinced that Rolfing should become my new career, I applied to study with Dr. Rolf and worked with her until her death in 1979. I continue to apply her teaching every day.

Rolfing is a process of deep-tissue manipulation, working primarily with the soft tissues of the body. Through

Rolfing, my work with athletes took on a whole new dimension. I discovered that when they were able to release unnecessary "holding patterns" or contractions in their body movements, and when their muscles were lengthened and made more resilient and responsive, their physiological efficiency and performance improved. When the physical structure is unrestricted by shortened muscles, scar tissues or imbalance around the joints and hinges of the body, then each part of the body is free to respond; a dynamic partnership is created within the body itself.

My studies with Ida Rolf taught me that life is expansion, and that living fully means moving in a free, expanded way. However, physical trauma, illness and accidents, not to mention just plain gravity, constantly tug us down, forcing our bodies to adjust by armoring, splinting and contracting. Through the practice of Rolfing, I discovered a way to open up the body, to give it freedom.

Ida Rolf, like Aristotle, believed in the inter-relationship between the body and the mind. Indeed, mental trauma can affect the body as severely as physical trauma. When children are frightened, their muscles contract and they learn to hold back, to move in a contracted manner. Memories of this sort—in fact, all memories and all experiences—are stored somewhere in the tissues of the body, affecting how we use our bodies for the rest of our lives. Each person holds memories in a different way, in a different part of the body. In my experience as a Rolfer, I have discovered that many memories surface during Rolfing sessions, and people recall incidents that happened to them early in their lives, incidents that they have long since forgotten.

Rolfing, then, as a physical way of reaching these experiences from the past, shares a goal with traditional psychotherapy: to bring the body and the mind into harmony. As a Rolfer, I approach therapy through body work. During 25 years of virtually unwrapping muscular armoring and re-balancing people's bodies, I learned that beneath the covering is always ease, balance and joy. This essential joy is trapped underneath a layer of conditioning, habits and physical compensations, with their resultant movement and behavior patterns. These layers upon layers of conditioned responses keep us from realizing our full potential and happiness. We have become what we believed our environment wanted.

I discovered that people can go through all types of emotional and mental therapy, but until they actually deal directly with the release of contractions in their physical bodies, they can still be "stuck." Yet when their bodies, are eased and the restrictions—the armoring, splinting and contracting—released, they move with greater resilience; then their perceptions, their minds and their lives also become more resilient.

Many of my clients report that as their physical constrictions and bindings get released, their hearts open and they experience greater feelings of loving. As layers of hurt, pain and negative experiences are unwrapped, it is easier to experience the deep loving that is inherent within all of us.

In this marriage of mind and emotions with the body, the relationship is, of course, reciprocal. Your emotions are powerful patterns that can work for or against you. Your emotions can affect the functioning and ultimately the structure of your body.

For example, if there is constant worry, then some part of your body will reflect that tension, usually through a contraction and shortening of the soft tissue and a resulting change in the posture and shape of your body. If you are angry, that anger will be reflected somewhere in your body, resulting in a particular way of moving. Over time, if that pattern is reinforced, it becomes permanent. If that movement pattern happens to put stress on an area of the body because of the interaction of the force of gravity with that movement, then it sets up symptoms of chronic discomfort. Each emotion affects the body in a unique way that is interfaced with your attitude. Your entire body, in a sense, is a mass of responses from your emotional make-up.

Conversely, the way you hold your body affects the way you respond emotionally. If the body is not resilient and free, that restriction affects attitude, perception and emotional make-up. For example, if your physical structure does not support you and you slouch, that can create an attitude of depression and lowered self-esteem. Your entire emotional climate goes into a slump. If you work with the physical structure so that it provides more support, it creates a corresponding change in attitude that is more upright, allowing greater self-esteem. It is important to realize that this is a structural change which supports a postural change. Ida Rolf would say, "Posture is *doing* and structure is *being*." When you posture yourself, you are using energy to force your muscles to act in a certain way. If your structure is aligned and balanced, there is nothing to *do* with your posture. The structurally supported body conserves energy and creates a feeling of lightness and "upness." The posturing body, with habitual holding patterns, reflects attitudes and also creates emotions and perceptions, congruent with the holding posture of the body.

The way your body is structured or postured affects your emotions; your emotions and behavior affect the posture and, ultimately, the structure of your body. It is easy to see how physical movement patterns and emotional behavior patterns can reinforce each other, for better or for worse, in unending cycles.

A happy "marriage" requires body, mind and emotions working harmoniously together. If any one aspect is out of synchronization, it affects the other aspects and there is a disharmony that can lead to dis-ease. The body is the most tangible part of your complex nature, something you can get your hands on in a three-dimensional world. You can change the quality of the body and its function, and thereby alter mental, emotional and spiritual levels to the relative degree that the body has changed. Although by using your mind you can change your body, it is the actual focus on the physical that will change it most rapidly. If you focus on creating ease in the mind, the body will slowly change to match that focus, but the holding patterns already in the body will limit your development.

The body must be re-educated in a direct way to make real progress. We can retrain the body, through exercise and new, deliberately chosen movement patterns. If you focus on creating the partnership within your body, and use your mind to assist that process, the progression will be much more rapid. The body can be used as a tool to alter all other aspects of yourself. The way you walk, sit and move physically can be used to change your attitudes and the way you function in the world.

In any marriage, honesty and integrity are ground rules for a happy relationship. Unfortunately, many of us end up lying to our bodies. How many times have you been angry or upset at someone and forced a smile onto your face, forced your body language to be a picture of congeniality? This incongruity between your emotions and your physical responses is basically a lie. However, your body is not so easily deceived. What happens over time is a breach of trust between you and your body, and your marriage is headed for the rocks.

In performance workshops these incongruities become very apparent. Emotions arise that are often hard to accept, much less express, creating tension in the body. During performance coaching, as I encourage the body to release its tension, the emotion usually changes in a positive way.

I remember one rehearsal with Stephanie, a petite, well-groomed lawyer in her late 20s. This was her first solo stage performance, and I could feel her anxiety as she moved to center stage. She stood with knees locked, feet nailed to the stage floor. Her arms held stiffly at her sides, she began to sing in a voice that sounded like it was being strangled somewhere back in the recesses of her throat. She was right on pitch, though, and never missed a word. Yet halfway through the performance her voice started to quiver and tears began to surface from the tension of pretending that she wasn't afraid.

"Stephanie," I stopped her. "What are you feeling right now?"

"Nervous and scared," she said between sobs. "And foolish."

"How does your body feel right now?" I asked.

"Shaky," she replied.

"Stephanie," I coached, "I'd like you to sing your song again and this time I want you to shake your body all over while you're singing. Just let your body shake as much as it wants to."

She looked at me in disbelief, but somehow mustered the courage to do it anyway. As she sang and shook, the tension in her knees relaxed. She shook her arms wildly and let her pelvis rock back and forth. Gradually, the tightness in her throat subsided and a clear, resonant voice emerged.

"I can sing!" she shouted when it was all over, shaking now from excitement rather than fear.

"That was really hard," she confessed. "All of my training kept running through my head and I kept thinking how ridiculous I must look. 'You have to be professional,' my mind kept saying. Yet when I shook, when I let my body do what it really wanted to do, the singing came much easier."

Stephanie admitted that she was anxious much of her life about other people's opinions of her performance—in college, in her profession, in her marriage. She held herself back from trying new things because of this fear of humiliation. This stage-singing experience taught her a lesson—a lesson learned deeply, imbedded in the cells of her body. By allowing her emotions to be what they were, and in the process, to let her body go, Stephanie experienced real partnership between her body and her emotions. The result was a successful performance. She now uses this experience of risking to express her emotions more fully in other areas of her life.

Again, any presentation—stage-singing, a business meeting, a party—can be a place where we exercise this choice to feel and express authentically. It may be some moment as simple as a conversation with a friend in a supermarket. Whatever the situation or circumstance, the issue is to become aware and responsive, and to tell that truth with both mind and body. When we stop trying to lie to ourselves and allow congruency between our emotions and our physicality, gradually the trust is restored in our broken marriage with the body. It is necessary to keep expressing, communicating, acting and being authentic so that there is minimal discrepancy between what you feel, think and do. In this way harmony is created at each moment. The extent to which you allow your body to express freely, along with your willingness to share yourself and your emotions—tears, laughter, sadness, excitement—at any single moment, dictate the level of joy and peace you experience in your life.

When you have reestablished trust between you and your body, that harmony will pervade all of your other relationships as well. The outer circumstances of our lives inevitably reflect our inner reality. *As a person thinks in the heart, so is he* is an ancient bit of wisdom that resonates through every life. We've all known people who just seemed accident-prone. I've been impressed with how often these people say things such as, "You just can't win." On the other hand, there are people who have suffered tremendous problems in life—traumatic childhoods, serious diseases—who somehow still find plenty of lucky breaks along the way. They become successes anyway. There is a level of willingness in such lives that makes it possible for the universe to support them through difficulties to joy.

In order for your body to believe you're sincere about making this marriage work, one more ingredient is essential. You must keep your agreements. Often we have great intentions but are short on follow-through. How many times have you promised yourself you would take a vacation, start a diet or begin an exercise program, only to find these promises lost in the fast-track of daily priorities? If you make promises to people that you fail to keep, they learn, after time, not to trust you. The same thing happens with your body. Interestingly enough, the body makes no distinctions between the simple and the grandiose promise. A promised trip to Tahiti is no more or less significant to the body than your promise to skip that fat-laden dessert tonight. The body holds you to your intention, every intention, no matter how seemingly small. If you want your marriage to work, you must follow your intentions with action.

When you've begun to reestablish trust in your marriage with your body, when the parts of the body are functioning as a synergistic team and your emotions, mind and body are working together harmoniously, then this personal foundation of harmony and partnership becomes the basis for partnership in your social relationships. When the body and emotions are in partnership, there is an ease and authenticity within yourself that communicates outwardly. People receive that harmony. The realness in your communications, in your body language, creates a charisma and magnetism that is hard to resist. When you've learned to trust yourself, people instantly feel you're a person they can trust. When you have successfully married your body, other partnerships are a natural progression.

BRING ON THE SKYHOOK: USING GRAVITY TO YOUR ADVANTAGE

Up to this point in time, humans have always developed and still live within the gravity pull of the earth. They must make their peace with this energy field, whatever it really is. To the extent that they fail to make peace and mistakenly carry on a war, gravity wins every time. The energy of this field can enhance or dissipate the energy of the individual. You cannot change the energy field but you can change the man.

—IDA P. ROLF

Gravity is a constant force. We are born into earth's field of gravity, and unless we become astronauts, we remain in this force field until we die. We seldom think about gravity, any more than a fish thinks about the ocean in which it swims. It is simply an unchanging part of our reality.

The effects of gravity, however, are all around us: in the slide of hillsides, in the rush of water down a stream, in the fall of Newton's proverbial apple. In architecture we see the effects of gravity in the stress of a poorly supported building. Over time, the cracks and slippage become self-evident.

In our bodies, too, the effects of gravity become self-evident. We usually blame it on aging, weakness or yard work, but in fact various painful and chronic symptoms are a direct result of gravity pushing down on the body, making it stressful for the body to hold itself up and function normally. If the structure is not aligned and balanced in a way that works with gravity, then the body will adapt and compensate in stressful ways in order to function. In time, the work expended in this compensation becomes too great and the burdened part of the body "gives out." You cry out, "My aching back!"—or shoulder, elbow, or neck—or you complain of tiredness and lack of energy. If you spend unnecessary energy just keeping upright and doing daily tasks, if your body is struggling to maintain its healthy function with the extra burden of gravity pushing down upon it in stressful ways, it's no wonder those aches and pains surface or those tired feelings take over.

Too many times we look at the body and its structure from a static position, looking for symmetry as the indication for balance. But how the body functions within that structure is probably more important than actual symmetry. Because the body is so adaptable and strives to be healthy and vigorous, it will make almost any kind of compensation to keep functioning. For example, your bony structure can be perfectly aligned, but if your musculature is not resilient enough to compensate for various stresses, you will have an "encased" body that does not move easily and spontaneously. Conversely, if the bony structure is misaligned, the muscles and soft tissue must work overtime to keep the body stabilized. The structure (your bones) and the soft tissue (everything else) have to work in partnership or there will be trouble. They are interdependent; without the proper support from both systems, chronic pain and discomfort arise.

As a Rolfer, I approach the body as an aggregate of individual sections (head, shoulders, chest, pelvis and legs), each with its own weight and balancing characteristics. The segmented body, when normal, is stacked like a series of blocks, one balanced on top of the other. Ida Rolf often used the analogy of the old-fashioned tent and the tent pole to help explain balance: What holds the tent up, the pole or the guy wires with their balanced tension on all sides of the pole? Of course, it's the guy wires. A balanced and aligned structure (body or tent) is relieved of the stress and tension of holding itself up. Bodies generally become unbalanced because of the combination of gravity with physical or emotional traumas. When one part of the body goes out of balance—a bone may become slightly displaced, leaving the muscle structures around it in a different position, for example—then other parts begin to compensate, and the way the body is stacked shifts. Some muscles shorten while others become rigid. Muscular fascial sheaths lose their ability to slide over each other. Eventually the body loses its freedom of movement, developing the symptoms, stresses and strains of a body that is losing its battle with gravity.

Many people spend enormous amounts of energy fighting their bodies. The body becomes a mass of compensations, and these compensations take their toll emotionally as well as physically. I recall one client, Diane, who, though she was only in her early 20s, complained of tiredness and chronic aching in her hip, shoulders and neck. She confessed that she felt ashamed of her body and disliked the way she looked. She felt irritable most of the time and was painfully shy. She told me that if someone said "hello" to her on the street, she turned away in fright.

As I looked at Diane's body I saw a mass of abnormal compensations. Her upper spine curved to the right. In order to compensate for this curvature, her pelvis had shifted to the left and her left knee was torqued inward to balance her body. She held her head tilted to the left, shortening the muscles in the left side of her neck. Other subtler compensations occurred throughout both sides of her body to maintain her balance in gravity. As this structure moved, her muscles were forced to compensate in order to support her body.

I began a series of Rolfing sessions with her to loosen the tightened and shortened muscles. As we balanced the muscle length throughout her body, the bony structure began aligning and the tension of the muscles on the bones began equalizing—just like guy wires on a tent. As her structure straightened and her muscles became more resilient, Diane's physical discomforts disappeared. She looked better and had greater confidence. She became much more communicative. After the sessions, she told me that she had started loving and accepting her body, and felt more joy in her life. As Diane's experience shows, when the body comes back into alignment, we literally feel as though a great weight has been lifted from our lives and our spirits.

I often observed that habitual body-movement patterns were reflected in my clients' personal and professional lives. One of my clients, John, a real estate broker, complained that no matter how hard he tried, he wasn't making any progress in his career. He also complained of lower-back pain. When I took a look at his walk the reason behind his lack of momentum was obvious. John swayed from side to side as he walked, leaning backward from the waist. It was if the bottom half of his body was moving faster than the upper half. He was going forward, but holding back at the same time. If you think you have an intention of doing one thing and your body is doing something else, an incongruity results—a lack of harmony, a discrepancy and confusion. This cross-purpose movement had translated into his professional life, blocking the forward momentum of his career. Exercising reinforced John's habits of movement, actually strengthening the muscles that had become shortened and thickened. If John did not become aware of the pattern, he would go on strengthening the cross-purpose movement.

I worked with John, showing him how he was moving and giving him several movement patterns he could practice. Primarily, I coached him to experience walking 100 percent in the direction he was going. As John began moving in one direction, his intention was reflected in his walk and movement. He became more confident, his sales doubled and his career started moving forward.

John told me that he felt his awkward walk and movement patterns came from his childhood, when he heard over and over again, "Stand up straight!" or "Successful people stand erect." There is, of course, nothing wrong with standing up straight, but erectness needs to come from a bony structure that is aligned and balanced to work *with* gravity, not from muscles working overtime to hold the body up. We all pick up ideas about how we should sit, stand, walk and move from parents, teachers, bosses—even from advertising. Many times this is damaging because we end up modeling other people's movement patterns as if they were our own. Others may think that what they teach us is perfectly appropriate for our bodies, but in doing so, they unknowingly rob us of our inner-awareness. It is only through a process of self-discovery, in movement as in all aspects of our lives, that we can express what is true for ourselves as individuals. *Know thyself* is essential physically, as well as spiritually, for a happy, healthy, productive life.

Part of the satisfaction I gain from teaching body ecology and movement seminars, as well as STAR Performance, is the joy of helping people discover the movement patterns that are right for them and their unique body structure. In the process the students often open up a new awareness of their God-given potential to be fully human—humorous, loving, sparkling and successful in their relationships with others.

When Karen, a strikingly beautiful woman with some prior stage experience, came to the workshop, she brought with her many preconceived ideas about how she should perform. Her song was emotionally powerful, yet her performance seemed contrived. She held her shoulders scrunched up toward her ears, with her stomach and pelvis tight, restricting the free flow of movement in her body. It looked painful, and I saw how much she was working against herself. I asked her to exaggerate the holding. When she realized the effect it was having on her spontaneity and how much stress it created, she let go. Now the intensity of her emotions could move freely throughout her entire body and also connect with her audience. The quality of her voice became much more dynamic. Her resulting ease, freedom and comfort were reflected in a stunning performance.

In observing Sam, another experienced singer, I noted that he puffed up his chest during his entire performance. Sam believed that "men keep their chests out." Furthering the pattern, his vocal teacher had trained him to contract his diaphragm to support the sound. The resulting holding pattern restricted the sound quality and prevented natural movement and resiliency in his body. He looked stiff and uncomfortable. I asked Sam to explore different ways of using his body as he sang by expressing various emotions: anger, sadness, joy. I told him to puff up his chest even more, then to let all of the air out of his lungs, depressing his chest completely. From this experience he learned what worked best for him and allowed his chest to settle downward as he sang, releasing the resistance against gravity. Immediately his sound was richer. He felt and looked more at ease, allowing the audience to relax and be at ease with him. His teacher meant well, and for some students the advice might have opened up a perfect way of singing. But all too often, we take "expert" advice and apply it wholesale to ourselves without testing it out against our own experience. In Sam's case, trying to fit a model, without taking into account his own experience, cut him off from himself and others.

Most communication is actually nonverbal. According to a study conducted by U.C.L.A. psychologist Albert Lorranian, only 7 percent of any communication takes place with words. At least 55 percent of a communication is made through your facial expression alone. So the way you use your body may communicate more than the words you say. If your body is tight and your movements are rigid, you are communicating something quite different than if your body is resilient and responsive. Gravity can be your enemy or your ally. Give gravity its due—but don't fight it.

To see how you respond to gravity, try this:

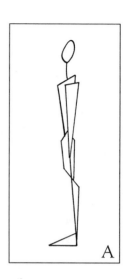

1. Stand up with your feet flat on the floor at shoulder width. Now rock forward from your ankles, over the balls of your feet, and hold that position. Notice which muscles you contract to keep you from falling on your face. Rock back to a standing position (fig. A).

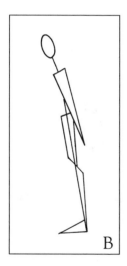

2. Rock forward again, this time noticing the position of your arms. If you are like most people, you probably held your arms back, as if doing so would keep you from falling (fig. B).

Try rocking forward again, this time letting your arms swing forward freely (fig. C).

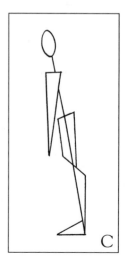

3. Now rock forward once more, again holding your arms back. Notice the difference in the way your body feels with each movement.

Holding your arms back is unnecessary and not in partnership with gravity as your momentum moves forward. If you can get out of the way and allow your body to cooperate with gravity and the force of your own momentum, then your body is under less stress and your movements communicate ease. Most of us go through life unaware of these unnecessary holding patterns formed in places where we restrict the freedom of movement in our bodies in an attempt to resist gravity. We go through our days unaware of the thousands of little unnecessary stresses, like holding our arms back when we walk, that create sore necks and shoulders or leave us tired at the end of the day. With some awareness, we can modify our movement patterns in any activity to relieve chronic discomfort, and create more energy and greater ease in our lives.

Much of our conceptual reference points about our bodies date back to classical Rome and Greece. These were the days when men went into battle or athletic events wearing armor. Tighter, more taut bodies were needed to support the weight of this armor. The days of centurions, or even of knights in shining armor, are gone, and our 20th-century lifestyle is more fluid. Our bodies need to be flexible and resilient, not muscle-bound and rigid. Yet ideas are slow to die, and much of our cultural body image is still in the middle ages.

BE A RAG DOLL

Try this: For one week give yourself permission to be sloppy and let go. Allow your shoulders to droop. Become a rag doll if you want to. Don't hold. Let the old patterns go.

LEARNING TO WALK

Now that you've cleared out your old patterns of movement and are ready to learn new ones, let's begin by learning how to walk.

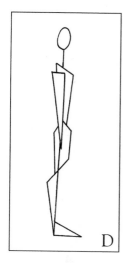

D

1. From a standing position (fig. D), rock forward as in the previous exercise, but this time let your leg swing forward freely from the hip socket as you take a step (fig. E).

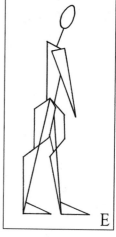

E

2. Let momentum and gravity carry you forward.

3. Let there be a slight forward lean to your body.

4. Allow yourself to move with a sense of "forwardness." This may feel a bit unusual at first. Many of us were taught that the proper way to walk was as if we were balancing a book on our heads. Walking like this puts your torso on hold and your legs have to work to pull you forward. When you let your entire body participate in the forward motion, gravity pulls you forward (E1).

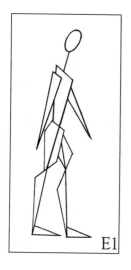

E1

The difference is subtle, but you will find that walking in this way takes much less energy. Once you have relearned how to walk, try applying these same principles to other movements, like jogging. When you make friends with gravity, it will become your ally and you will find yourself moving more in harmony with the earth.

BRING ON THE SKYHOOK!

Now that you're in touch with the earth and its gravitational pull, let's get in touch with heaven. Bring on the skyhook! Stand up and imagine a series of horizontal lines running throughout your entire body, about 1/2 inch apart from each other (fig. F).

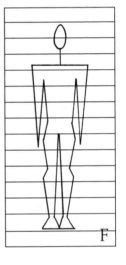

Now envision a line that runs in front of your spine and behind your throat, then up through the top of your head. Attach that line to a handy skyhook. Feel the skyhook pull you up toward heaven. Let the skyhook hold your head up and allow the rest of your body to rest down on the horizontal lines so that each segment supports the one above it, all the way down to the earth (fig. G). Now you are resting on the earth and letting the skyhook pull you up toward heaven. You are supported, from both worlds. Gravity is your ally, no longer your enemy, and your movement through space is effortless.

Capture this feeling, bring it into your conscious

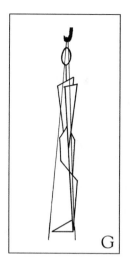

awareness, and notice when you move whether you are cooperating with gravity or resisting it.

Try using the skyhook exercise when you are sitting. Find your "sit bones" (ischial tuberosities) by sitting on your hands, palms up. Wiggle a little and feel the bones protruding. These bones support your spine, and you (fig. H).

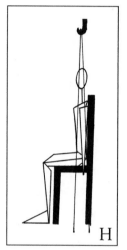

When you sit in a chair, be sure to slide your "sit bones" as far back in the chair as possible. Let the skyhook pull your head up, and allow the rest of your body to sink down, supported by each horizontal segment, until you are resting on your "sit bones" in the same way you would rest on your feet (fig. I).

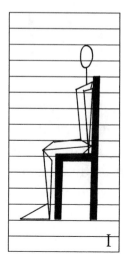

100 PERCENT PARTICIPATION

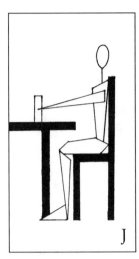

J

Sit down at a table with a glass of water slightly more than an arm's length away. Reach out for the glass (fig. J). Which parts of your body are you using to pick up the glass? Is your arm the only part of your body that's working, leaving the rest of your body on hold? Try it again, using your entire body in the action of picking up the glass. Rock your body forward from your pelvis, moving your whole torso toward the glass (fig. K). Now rock back to a sitting position.

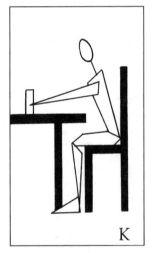

K

Take this awareness into other daily tasks (like hammering a nail or washing a floor), remembering to allow your whole body to partic-ipate in each movement, rather than putting one part of the body on hold while another part moves. Remember, any time you put part of your body on hold, you create tension.

These exercises are examples of what I like to call "body ecology." It's an awareness of ease and efficiency in your body movements that becomes a way of life. When you learn to use only necessary holding against gravity, and to utilize your own momentum in movement, then this partnership with gravity brings ease into your life. That ease is communicated in everything you do, bringing greater freedom, creativity and authenticity to your everyday performance. Going public with your dreams and abilities, accepting your stardom, doesn't mean adding stress to your life. It means releasing yourself in living more fully.

THE WIGGLE IN THE WALK: FREEING UP THE PELVIS

The pelvis has been called the cornerstone of the body. Variations in the alignment of the pelvis affect every other part of the body. One of the main directions in Rolfing is to align and balance the pelvis. The body will compensate and adjust for any distortion in the pelvis, and therefore the alignment of the pelvis affects how your body moves as well as how you feel. Muscular contractions are the main cause of the imbalances that lead to variations in alignment.

As a body therapist, I have observed literally thousands of people over the years and studied the ways they move. In so many cases, I have observed that people move as though their pelvis did not exist. There seems to be a case of cultural alienation when it comes to the pelvis. Because the pelvis contains the reproductive organs and organs of elimination, it is subject to all of the mental and emotional associations we have formed in these areas. In our culture, early toilet training leaves us with the association that this area of the body is something to be *controlled*. Further, elimination is done in private, which teaches us that the pelvis is not something to display. As we get older, conventional sexual morality reinforces the idea that this area of the body is private, and again, something to be controlled. Women are taught to posture themselves holding their legs together tightly. The connotations, messages and mores about the pelvis being sexual if moved cause parents to admonish their daughters to eliminate the wiggle in their walk for fear of being seen as *loose* women.

All of these cultural mores foster tightly held pelvises. I see people walking around daily with rigid pelvises that restrict the freedom of movement throughout their bodies. When movement is inhibited in this way, it can cause all manner of compensations in other areas of the body for the lack of pelvic movement. The adaptations made by other parts of the body create undue stress in specific areas and can, in time, create chronic symptoms of discomfort in the back, chest, shoulders, elbows, neck, or legs and feet. Additionally, emotional discomfort as well as many maladies (such as sexual and elimination problems) can stem from a rigid pelvis.

In my private practice, I encourage my clients to put the wiggle back in their walk. As an exercise, I ask them to allow their pelvis to swing uninhibitedly as they walk. For many people, this is a difficult exercise. It brings up memories of parental admonitions and the fear that they will attract sexual advances they may not want. Very often, heterosexual men fear that if they allow their pelvis to move freely as they walk, someone will think they are homosexual. I tell them, " Do it anyway." When you allow yourself integrity of movement without regard for what others may think, you will discover a way of moving that works for you, not against you. My clients always report that after doing this exercise, they feel better both physically and mentally and have more energy. I believe that the gain in energy is from releasing the conditioned holding patterns in the pelvis, freeing it to move without restriction or tension. This allows the energy to flow freely from the pelvis throughout the body. As the pelvis becomes freer, the entire body responds; attitudes become freer and easier as well. Outlook becomes more positive; expression and movement become more authentic.

Viewing the pelvis anatomically, there is only one pair of muscles that directly crosses the pelvis from the torso to the legs: the psoas. If the psoas is in balance and allowed to work without restriction, then both the upper and lower parts of the body can move with greater responsiveness. As a Rolfer and movement teacher, I have used certain movements to effect greater freedom in the use of the psoas and the surrounding structures. In doing these exercises, it is not only the movements that are important, however; it is the conscious focus of your attention and your intent in very specific ways which will create the appropriate movements.

PELVIC ROCK

One of the exercises that will allow the psoas and the pelvis greater freedom is the pelvic rock, done with appropriate breathing. Try it now:

1. Lie down on your back, preferably on a soft carpet or thin foam pad. If your neck feels stressed or uncomfortable, fold a towel and tuck it under the back of your head (fig. L).

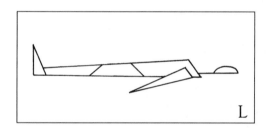

L

2. Begin to observe your breath and notice the rise and fall of your belly and chest.

3. Begin to focus on your exhale and slowly and easily allow more of your breath to be exhaled. Allow your ribs to move footward and floorward as you exhale. It is important not to force the air out, but to allow the ribs to let go as more air is exhaled. Let the inhale take care of itself. You will inhale automatically. Enjoy the release of any holding patterns that keep your ribs in an inflated or slightly inflated position. It is when you allow all of the old to expire that you allow the new to enter. As you do this with your breath, the mind

subconsciously responds and new thoughts and ideas can surface, bringing you greater creativity.

4. Now slide your feet along the ground toward your buttocks, resting with your feet flat on the floor and your knees bent facing the ceiling (fig. M).

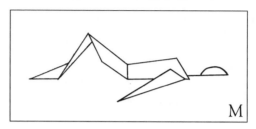

M

5. Continue your breathing, focusing on the exhale, but now feel your abdomen becoming very soft and let it rest floorward.

6. Carry this ease and softness into the bowl of your pelvis, and feel or sense the soft tissue of the inner pelvis as if it were a bowl of jelly. Allow your anal sphincter muscle to let go if it is holding tight. Experience the quiet and softness as you breathe, focusing on the exhale.

7. Now allow your pubic bones (the bones above your genitals) to gently raise toward your nose without lifting the pelvis or contracting the abdominal wall. You will find that as you do this properly, you will be pushing from the bottom of your feet and your knees will move slightly forward. It is important not to use the outer stomach muscles to do this. Rest your hands on your stomach so that you can feel if you are contracting those muscles.

8. Do these pelvic rocks 3-6 times, slowly and consciously.

SPATIAL DESIGN EXERCISES

The pelvic rock initiates the psoas directly and assists in creating balance and ease within the pelvic girdle. Essentially, it is a process of introducing new movement patterns which will allow greater ease of motion. The following spatial design exercises will also assist in making the pelvis more agile:

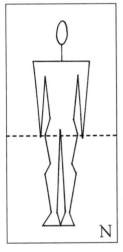

1. Do the pelvic rock while standing, keeping the knees soft and slightly bent. Imagine a line going through the center of your hip bones and through your body from right to left (fig. N). Bring your pubic bones forward around the line and up toward your nose, then back down toward the ground. Do this slowly (fig. O).

2. Now, move the pelvis to the right and then to the left, letting it rotate around an imaginary line going through your pelvis from front to back.

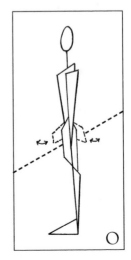

3. Do hip circles, moving only the pelvis, with the torso and legs remaining relatively stable.

4. Figure eights: make the shape of a capital D with your pelvis to one side, then the other.

In doing these spatial design exercises, allow your body to respond to the pelvic movements while keeping the knees soft.

These movements, although simple, are powerful. According to Dr. Rolf, beneath the sacrum is the Ganglion of Impar, an area where the sympathetic and parasympathetic (voluntary and involuntary) nervous systems join. When this area is stimulated, there is a subjective feeling of well-being. When the pelvis moves freely in all directions, the Ganglion of Impar is stimulated, giving you a greater opportunity to feel good, as well as to communicate with greater gusto and believability.

In STAR Performance trainings, I discovered that in working with these movement exercises and in bringing greater conscious awareness to the pelvic area, participants dramatically released holding patterns and tensions in their pelvises, and in so doing, were able to release tension in other parts of their bodies as well. As their bodies became more fluid, so did their expression, and their communications were much more believable. Freeing up movement in the pelvis is critical to congruency between mind and body. It allows energy to flow freely between the upper and lower parts of your body. Removing obstructions in the pelvic area can allow your entire body to be more responsive, freeing your communication and allowing your charisma to unfold.

Yes, you may get some attention as a result of your new way of moving, or perhaps just because of your new comfort in your body. You may find that attention disquieting at first, especially if someone expresses a negative opinion. Remind yourself that an opinion is only an opinion, not fact. Being comfortable in your own body is a long way from being "loose" or "promiscuous." For every negative opinion you get, you'll probably find several more people who are delighted to meet a more complete you. And all the energy you'll free up for work and play will convince you that it was a fair trade.

BREAKING THE
COMFORT BARRIER

Fear is the mind killer. Fear is the little death that brings total obliteration. I will face my fear. I will permit it to pass over me and through me. And when it has gone past me I will turn to see fear's path. Where the fear has gone there will be nothing. Only I will remain.

—FRANK HERBERT
"BENE GESSERIT LITANY", *DUNE*

Fear is our jailer. It is fear that limits us, that sets the boundaries of our lives beyond which we may not pass. Most of us live within these boundaries, content with the security of our comfortable lives, never confronting the jailer that stalks us, rearing his ghoulish face when we dare to cross the comfort barrier.

I'm not talking about jumping out of airplanes, crossing Niagara Falls in a barrel or climbing the Himalayas. It is not daredevil acts that are required of us in order to escape our self-maintained prison. Rather, it is a willingness to take small risks, to stretch the boundaries of what we are comfortable in expressing about ourselves, to challenge ourselves to explore our own potential and to let others see the star that lies within us.

In general, physical risks are not as transformative as psychic or emotional risks. Revealing our inner selves can be more frightening than exposing ourselves to physical danger. Today it is not pitting our bodies and wills against the challenges of nature; it is our interaction with other people that provides the arena in which we conquer our fears. In today's world, competition is stiff. In order to land that promotion, attract that new client or get that hot job offer, you must be very visible. Being visible requires taking risks in your self-expression. Successful people are not afraid of taking risks. They know what's on the other side of risking; the pay-off is worth the leap into the unknown and the uncomfortable.

Risks vary from person to person. What feels unbearably risky to one person may be totally comfortable to another. We must each discover where we have drawn our comfort barriers and what will push us past them. If you feel comfortable taking the next step in your path, then you need a bigger step. When you start feeling uncomfortable, you're on the right track. Then, stretch yourself a little further. When that cold ember of fear starts to spark and burn in your guts, you're on the road to a personal breakthrough. Keep going! There's no limit to how far you can go if you're willing to face your fears and battle your discomfort and uncertainty.

Often when we look at successful or particularly courageous people, we assume they have enjoyed this sort of confidence all their lives. Not necessarily so. Take Gandhi, for example. No one doubts the extraordinary courage of this humble, solitary individual who challenged injustice with nonviolence and led an entire nation to freedom. In his eulogy of Gandhi, Albert Einstein said, "Generations to come will scarce believe that such a one as this ever in flesh and blood walked upon this earth."

Yet Gandhi's early years were filled with self-inflicted terror. He was afraid of the dark, and wrote that as a schoolboy, he was very shy and could not bear to talk to anybody. Later, as a young lawyer, Gandhi found himself completely helpless in the courtroom. Recalling the first time he started to cross-examine a witness, he said that his head reeled and he couldn't get a word out. He sat down and could not continue with the case.[1]

What was it that pushed Gandhi past his fears, that broke his personal comfort barrier? Alone in South Africa, miles from his wife and family, Gandhi was working as a translator in a law firm. He watched as fellow Indians were daily thrashed and continually insulted by Europeans. He was shocked and intimidated and wanted nothing more than to go back to India. Late one night a European police

---

1. "Gandhi: The Evolution of a Soul," *Heart* III:2 (Autumn 1983), 9.

constable pushed him out of the train in which he was riding. As he sat in the train station through the long cold night, shivering and meditating, his principles triumphed over his fears. He decided he would not run away, but would stay to complete what he had undertaken. Gandhi's dedication to truth and justice gave him strength to persevere where few others would have had the courage to continue. His experiences in South Africa became a training ground for the massive nonviolent resistance movement he would later organize in his native India.

Life presents us, like Gandhi, opportunities to overcome our fears, to stretch ourselves past our limits. How we respond to these opportunities is the true test of our dedication to living our lives fully. Are you courting life like a lover, drawing from it the challenges that will free your spirit, or are you hiding away in your room while life passes by like a beautiful person casting a shadow on the wall of your prison?

In STAR Performance, I have seen dramatic personal transformations that come from a willingness to risk. Once that comfort barrier is broken, and the possibility of freedom exists, new life starts to animate the personality. The real star begins to shine through.

When Alan walked through the door to one of my workshops, he was shy and soft-spoken, often looking at the ground as he talked. He was a good-looking man in his mid-30s with a well-proportioned body and a beautiful smile. He had come to the workshop on the recommendation of a friend who was a STAR graduate, strictly as an act of faith.

Alan was ending a long struggle with alcohol and drug addiction. He had spent several years in prison and was just beginning to turn his life around. When he got up to perform, Alan would not look at the audience, nor would he look at me. He started singing a song written by Cat Stevens. He sang about being miles from anywhere. He was singing about his life, and becoming increasingly emotional. He sang haltingly about looking up at the mountain he had to climb, while tears filled his eyes. Soon there was no melody to his song, no rhythm, simply pure emotion. I asked him to keep singing through his tears. He sang to the floor. He sang to the wall. Finally he had enough courage to sing to one person, looking into his eyes. He sang about having his freedom and making his own rules. He had broken the comfort barrier and touched one person with his song, with himself.

By the end of the workshop Alan was singing solo in front of a room full of people. He sang from the depths of his heart, and the sincerity of his message blazed through the audience like a prairie fire. He had achieved his freedom and took his audience right out the prison door with him. It was one of the most electrifying performances I have ever witnessed.

Remember my father—the one who had banned music from my childhood? Needless to say, he had not sung once in his 72 years, not even in the shower. He was visiting me one weekend when I was teaching a STAR Performance workshop and I talked him into participating. I realized I was pushing him way past his comfort barrier into territory he'd never even considered exploring.

He remembered a song he had loved as a young man when he was just starting to date my mother. He bought the record and listened to it over and over again to learn the words and the tune. The night of the performance, I have to admit I held my breath as I watched him walk slowly onto the stage. He dedicated his song "All of me" to my mother, who had died less than a year previously. His eyes glistening, he sang for her to take all of him. His message was clear: He was giving all of himself and the audience loved him for it. I noticed I wasn't the only one who was crying.

I watched my father's life change after that performance. He loved to go on senior citizen tours to Las Vegas. My father was a shy man, but I heard from a friend of his that he had stood in the middle of the tour bus and started singing. Soon he was leading the entire bus in a sing-along.

I am continually amazed at the degree of tyranny that fear can have in people's lives, and even more amazed at how easily that tyranny can be broken, once people are willing to trust their own innate ability to adapt, to persevere. When I first met Sally—a slender, spritely girl with a head full of strawberry-blonde curls—she was so shy that she wouldn't even call up a restaurant to make a dinner reservation. She was so afraid of other people's opinions of her that even a stranger on the other end of a phone line was intimidating. For Sally, solo stage singing was light years beyond her comfort barrier.

The night of the public concert for STAR Performance she stood up on stage, knees visibly shaking. Through her tears, she sang the Whitney Houston song "The Greatest Love of All" about loving yourself being the most important kind of love. Sally *was* learning to love herself, perhaps for the first time in her life. She swallowed hard after every line, singing off-key and out of rhythm, but with a steadfast determination not to stop until she had made it through that song. For Sally, the goal was not a stunning performance, but simply the willingness to perform at all. The audience was not concerned with the quality of her voice or her stage presence, but simply with her courage to face them and be herself. They gave her a standing ovation—not for her singing, but for her victory over intimidation.

A few weeks after that performance I was walking on a beach. I rounded a bend and recognized that head of blond curls. There was the girl who couldn't even speak to a stranger on the phone, smiling and talking animatedly with a group of young men.

For other, more gregarious people, the comfort barrier may be a certain style or a fixed idea about their daily "performance." For them, the risk is trying out new ways of expressing themselves, even if it feels uncomfortable. Sometimes that process requires going to extremes, just to break up crystallized styles of behavior.

I remember coaching Robert, a muscular, attractive man in his mid-30s who worked in a recording studio. He confessed that he had always wanted to be on the other side of the microphone, performing. During rehearsal his performance was rote and mechanical. He was doing what he thought a singer should do, but there was no life in his song. He had a good voice, yet it lacked force or authority.

I asked him to sing the song like Hitler might have done. He looked at me with an incredulous expression and asked:

"Adolf Hitler singing 'The Rose'?"

But he did it anyway. Holding two fingers under his nose to simulate a mustache, he goose-stepped across the stage. He sang in a strong, deep voice, clipping his words to the staccato beat of his march. Somewhere toward the end of his "Hitler" performance I watched a breakthrough occur. He had pushed himself past his comfort barrier and gotten a taste of power, of authority. When he returned to his former style, something had changed. His voice was clear and direct, his movements self-assured. His song had come to life with new meaning that had arisen from a deeper place within him, the center of his own power.

One of the most endearing performances I have witnessed during the STAR concerts came from a young black woman with a voice as rich as her enthusiasm for life. Serena was definitely beautiful—she stood a full 5 feet 8 inches with a face that radiated vitality—and she wanted to sing "beautiful." I asked her to sing "unbeautiful." She had fixed ideas about her style. I wanted to widen her vocabulary, to show her that there was more than one way to sing the same song. She wanted to sing sweetly; I had her sing like Ethel Merman. She wanted to be a serious performer; I had her sing on her hands and knees wagging her tail. For Serena, being dignified and serious about herself and her performance was comfortable. To stretch her beyond her comfort barrier required getting her to be a comedian, to laugh at herself and to make others laugh with her.

Breaking up the crystallization in the style of Serena's performance also broke down the barriers in her relationships. Suddenly there was nowhere to hide, and she realized how much energy she had spent maintaining her dignity while keeping everyone else at arm's length.

Her final performance was captivating. With the conviction of one who knows, she sang "People," a song that tells why people who need others are lucky. The range of emotional expression she brought to that song rivaled even that of Barbra Streisand. Her face was as vibrant as the yellow and gold African caftan she wore. She sang from her soul: She sang from her soul that she used to be incomplete, but now she was complete. Her stage presence carried to the back of the room, leaving no one untouched. After her standing ovation she said, "I've been singing all my life, but I never really sang until tonight!"

The range of people's fears and comfort barriers are as varied as the life experiences that created them. The requirements of each person's process are unique. Only you know when you are really pushing yourself and when you are simply skirting the edges of what's comfortable for you. Here are some practical suggestions, a risk-taking primer to help you take that inevitable leap past the security of your own comfort zone:

1. Make a list of each aspect of your life: your relationships, your career, your recreational interests, your financial situation, your spiritual life. Using a separate sheet of paper for each part of your life, write the name of that aspect at the top of the page. Then spend five to ten minutes sitting quietly with your thoughts about it. What comes up for you? "I wish I could . . . I wish I had . . . I want . . . I feel . . .

I really like . . . I fear . . . I should . . ." Jot down whatever thoughts or phrases come up for you. Here's a tip: When something comes up that gets an automatic "Oh, I can't write *that*" or "That's not nice!"—then you're really onto something important. Make yourself write it down. It won't hurt you (or your mother, father, spouse or God) just to write it down.

This is like taking an inventory in a store. You don't *have* to do anything with what you find, but it's possible you'll find something very valuable hidden behind that counter. You can decide what to do with it later. Right now you're just looking. So write it down. Then you may want to put it away for a day or two, and tend to your daily life while your subconscious thinks about what you wrote.

2. Okay, now you're ready to look at it again. Here's the key: When you find yourself saying "I want . . ." or "I need . . . ," realize that those phrases are valuable clues to your next step to happiness. If you found yourself writing "I want to learn to fly," label another sheet "Flying" at the top of the page. Each day, fill in one line on the page with one step you have made toward that goal. It could be simply calling to find out the cost of flying lessons, or who gives lessons in your town. (Don't worry yet about how to pay for the lessons; just make the call!) Another step could be going to the library to read *Flying Magazine*, or ordering a subscription. Remember, tiny steps count, too. I

promise you—by the time you get to the bottom of the page, you'll know a lot more about flying, and you will be on the way to that goal. More importantly, you'll be learning about pushing through your comfort barriers. You'll be taking little risks that will break down that wall into surmountable little hurdles.

Often it is not fear of failure that stops us from taking risks, but a secret fear of success. Our self-talk may convince us that our present environment is safer, and that a new situation will feel strange and uncomfortable. Let yourself daydream what it would feel like to be president of the company, a captivating public speaker or a professional tennis player. Whatever your dream, make it vivid. Imagine your office, the smooth grain of the mahogany desk, the rich color of the curtains. Or imagine the feeling you get from that round of enthusiastic applause at the end of your speech, or the cheers of the crowd as you ace a tournament tennis game. There is no quota on successful people; you deserve success as much as the next person. Set aside some time every day to dream. Make it as real as possible. Write it down in as much detail as possible. You are teaching yourself to believe, and your actions will surely follow your belief.

3. Enlist a friend or two to be your personal support team. Let them know you're planning on taking some new risks in your life and you'd like their help. Tell them you'll be calling them when your courage is

waning—it may. Ask them to urge you to "do it any-way," no matter how many excuses or long lists of fears you recite.

4. Remind yourself often—even daily—of the pay-off and why it's worth taking this risk. Ask yourself: What will my life be like if I don't take this risk?

5. Look back at your notes about your life. Notice those places where you wrote something like "I should . . ." or "I ought to . . ." or "I ought *not* . . . I shouldn't . . ." Here's a very important thing I have learned at great expense, and I'm passing it on to you free of any extra charge: Whenever I am using the words "I ought" or "I should," it is a dead giveaway that I am not in real-ity anymore. That's my grandmother or a minister or a teacher or somebody else talking, not me! It means I have stopped listening to my own heart, and it means I'm getting myself into trouble. That is espe-cially true if I attach any of those phrases to my feel-ings. "Oh, I shouldn't want nicer clothes; it wouldn't be the spiritual way to spend money. . . . I shouldn't feel angry about that. . . . I shouldn't want to quit this job when I'm lucky to have a job at all. . . ."

You and I are entitled to our feelings. We may choose not to act on them right away—I may not choose to quit my job until I have a new and more congenial one lined up—but to ignore or deny our feelings is a quick route to a hell-ish life. And to give anyone else free rent in my head means

I'm living someone else's life, not my own. Discard any considerations you may have about what other people think about your goals and aspirations. You're taking these risks for you, not for them. What really matters is what you think of yourself. You may want to spend some time writing out what you think specific others say, or might say, about your dreams and efforts. Then imagine and write down the strongest response you can imagine to them. Your list might look like this:

> Dad: Why are you wasting your time on school? You're pretty enough; you don't need a Ph.D.

> Me: It's enough that I want it! My time isn't wasted, it's invested in a new life of joy and achievement. And yes, I am pretty enough to do whatever I want, and I'm smart enough, too!

> Frank: Sis, when are you going to find a man and settle down? Or at least get a real job?

> Me: Right now, my job is studying. Since you're not paying my tuition, the rest of it is none of your business.

Find whatever phrases you are comfortable with and practice them. Oddly enough, you may find you never have to actually use them. Once we get comfortable with ourselves and our dreams, other people seem to instinctively know it. You may find that the people whose opinions you feared turn out to be your biggest cheerleaders!

A STAR Graduate

I learned how to risk in a fun-loving day
I came from my heart and it showed me the way
I knew there was tenseness and holding, not ease
So he made me forget and get down on my knees
I rolled on my stomach and then on my back
I felt so damn foolish for the things that I lack
It made me aware of the things in my life
How something so silly cuts in like a knife
I sang it again and this time for real
The audience giggled and I was so still
What wasn't working, I started to cry
That made me ask questions that started with why

The freedom to move if it's something you lack
It could be so restricting, it could injure your back
I was holding a pattern like unexpressed pain
That was written all over me, especially when I sang
I had a strange feeling that this was my thing the process had
stirred
And I was learning to sing.
I have learned so much from that very first day
And I'm learning to accept that I am okay.

Taking a risk only takes guts
And a very strong person who takes no short-cuts
Try it someday and "sing from your heart"
You try it just once and you'll be hooked from the start!

KAMERON, 20 YEARS OLD

OUTWITTING THE CRITICS: A DEBUTANTE'S GUIDE TO THE MIND

As we prepare to make our debut on life's stage, confronting our next public performance (no matter what the arena), inevitably we find ourselves beset by a cacophony of nagging voices coming from somewhere in the balcony. Charles Fillmore, a co-founder of Unity Church, used to call these voices "thought people." All too often our heads are full of these intangible but very real players. Depending on our individual life experiences, the cast of characters filling the peanut gallery of our minds will vary, but let's take a look at some of the archetypal figures that act as critics.

Even before we step onto the stage, we may be beset by a shady figure lurking in the wings—Bud Whatif. Bud is likely to be found slinking around the backstage dressing room, wringing his hands, his forehead contorted in a worried frown. As we contemplate our upcoming performance, he pokes his little bald head in the door and interjects a dire prediction of peril and failure.

"But what if you get fired?" he asks, as you're about to speak to your superior at work about a policy change. "How will you support yourself?" Or, as you are about to ask a friend to come with you to a concert, Bud speaks up: "But what if she thinks you're weird for being interested in Appalachian folk singing?" You have some concerns about a procedure at work, and Bud whispers, "But if you make the maintenance department mad, you'll never get this office cleaned again!"

If we listen too often to Bud, we'll find ourselves paralyzed by fear and hesitation. Any time we consider going public and taking a risk by expressing ourselves, there is the potential for both positive and negative feedback. In taking any risk we must weigh the potential for failure, criticism or loss against the potential benefits of the risk. But this has to happen in a realistic, present-time manner, not clouded by the hysteria of our negative conditioning from the past. Once we've made up our mind to "go public" and take a risk, then the best way to handle Bud Whatif is to grab him by the collar, look him in the eye and shout, "So what!"

Now that we've collared Bud and made our way out of the dressing room and onto the stage, we're exposed to the critics in the balcony. In the front row of the balcony, we're likely to find Auntie Goodenough, who may bear a startling resemblance to our first-grade teacher, nagging grandmother or childhood piano instructor. Looking over her spectacles, eyebrows raised and head cocked accusingly to one side, Auntie Goodenough surveys the scene with a critical glance, waiting to comment on any misstep. "You haven't memorized your lines thoroughly enough," she insists, as you're about to step on stage. "You're too young to be vice president of this company," she reminds you, as you're about to address the board meeting. "Nobody will take you seriously." You're about to go for a job interview, and she murmurs, "I guess that suit was the best you could find. Well, at least it almost covers up that spare tire you've developed." And then she whispers, "Don't worry, dear. I'll always love you even if no one else can see your good points. Don't forget to smile. You'd be pretty if you smiled more."

In short, Auntie Goodenough is that part of our self-talk that is quick to point out our inherent insufficiencies. If we listen to Auntie Goodenough, we will most likely wait in the wings until we have earned a Ph.D., taken voice lessons for at least five years, or researched our subject until our original enthusiasm is buried beneath facts and figures. While we are perfecting whatever aspect of ourselves just isn't good enough, opportunity passes us by.

If we survive Auntie Goodenough, however, we may still have to confront her close ally, John B. Good. Depending on our upbringing, John may appear in clerical collar, priest's vestment or judge's robes John B. Good is the ever-present censor, always on the lookout for actions or expressions that cross the boundaries of our social conditioning. He's the freedom squelcher. Just as we're about to do something totally new, we'll hear his gavel come down with a resounding "No!" Just as we're about to experiment with a unique mode of expression, his monotone litany of shoulds echoes through the sacred corridors of our mind:

"You should act properly."

"You'd better not embarrass your family."

"You'll look like a fool."

If we listen too closely to John B. Good, it is likely that the performance of our lives will stick to the same rote lines we have learned since childhood. Now that we've grown up, we're ready to make choices for ourselves, based on our own personal values—which may or may not correspond to those we've inherited. As we expand our horizons of expression, we may find ourselves shedding outmoded behaviors. Some of John's criticism may be valid; however, the point is to have a choice in what we do, not to be at the mercy of a censor operating in our subconscious. The most painful example of John at work may be the stories, familiar to many employees of rape crisis-centers, of women who numbly obeyed orders from attackers because they just wouldn't fight back. Trained to be "ladylike," they missed chances to defend themselves or flee. Some women beginning self-defense classes have found it difficult to learn to shout or scream to discourage aggressors.

Close behind John B. Good stands Colonel Should. His role is to demand that you do too many—often contradictory—things all at once. "You should," he nags in our mind's ear, "you should study . . . create the perfect birthday party for your six-year-old and his 30 closest friends . . . see that movie and read all the reviews . . . read that bestseller . . . meditate at least an hour a day . . . weave your own baskets like the creative woman in that magazine." It doesn't matter what task you have at hand; the colonel knows at least five better ways for you to spend your time, energy and money. As a friend of mine says, "Thou shalt not 'should' on yourself." You can drive yourself crazy trying to satisfy all those demands, and never enjoy any of your activities as a result.

Many people find that the colonel slowly vanishes if they use a simple, but not necessarily easy, tool. The tool is clarity of purpose. That may mean something as simple as making a list of three things you want to achieve today and doing them first, one at a time, until you finish. Many executives find that list-making is the most important management skill they ever acquire. For many of us, making a list doesn't quite do the job, because we haven't yet figured out our larger purpose. Each of us has a divine purpose in life, a reason we are here on earth. Some people seem to know that purpose almost from birth. Mozart is a good example. He started his music career as a child prodigy and poured out the compositions until he died. Some women seem to know from young childhood that they want to be full-time mothers and nurturers. Some people never doubt that they were born to be doctors or writers. Others of us flail around for years, not quite sure what we are doing here. For us, finding out what that divine purpose is may be our first priority. Once we know, then our activities can be centered around that purpose, and it becomes easier to ignore Colonel Should's pressure to dissipate our energies. The colonel can be demoted to buck private when you clarify what's important to you—for this hour, this day and this life. But how do we find that purpose?

To start, make a list of the things you do or have or that exist which make you excited and happy. It may be embroidery, writing, skiing or cooking. Do you prefer being alone or with people? Indoors or outdoors? Keep asking yourself what you like and what brings you joy. The answers will come, and each one will be a clue to your path.

Many people find, as they seek their path, that a consistent program of prayer and meditation makes the way clearer. Call it God, Divine Mind, Universal Intelligence, Higher Power, Tao or The Way—something out there responds when we ask questions, and the answers *do* come.

Keeping a journal and recording our daily experiences will help make the questions and answers clearer. Be patient. Remember that we are listening for a small voice that may come as an intuition, feeling or knowing—not as thunder.

The last of our cast of characters, though not as vociferous as the rest, is often the most insidious. Somewhere, probably snoozing in the back row of the balcony, we're likely to find Wanda B. Cozy. Wrapped tightly in her warm overcoat, a box of chocolates snuggled into her lap, she's content to ignore the show altogether as long as her seat is paid for. Wanda is the self-appointed Queen of Indifference, the guardian of the Comfort Zone. She is content to watch as you slumber through your daily routines, basking in the warm glow of unruffled security. But try a change of pace, and her protests go off like an alarm. "WARNING. WARNING. COMFORT ZONE HAS BEEN VIOLATED." Pretty soon she has Bud Whatif on the phone and they're conjuring up dire consequences and pumping a full-blown scenario into your cerebral cortex.

You can almost outline a formula for failure: You're tired of doing XYZ and you've decided to make a change and do ABC. As you're about to take a step toward ABC you find yourself wondering about possible negative consequences. Suddenly XYZ doesn't look so bad anymore and you wonder why you wanted to make a change in the first place.

Wanda is that part of ourselves that is unwilling to pass through that period of discomfort that almost always accompanies change. The best strategy for controlling Wanda is simply recognizing self-talk (or thought person) for what it is—an attempt to maintain comfort at the cost of self-actualization. Once you can recognize what is going on inside of you and ignore the warning signals Wanda transmits, you'll be able to break through the comfort barrier and achieve a higher level of personal freedom and expression.

With such a cast of characters crowding the balcony of our minds, it's no wonder that we often manage to talk ourselves out of doing anything that would outrage the

censors or get a rise out of the critics. If we listen to all
these voices, the performance of our lives will be limited
by the same considerations that we have played out since
childhood. But laughter is good medicine, and if we can
manage a humorous glimpse at the folly of our own objec-
tions and considerations, we may succeed in freeing ourselves of them altogether or at least in not allowing them
to run our lives. We can live fully in the midst of all the
voices. If you have "thought people" like Auntie
Goodenough, Bud Whatif, John B. Good or Wanda B.
Cozy lurking in the balcony, keep this Debutante's Guide
to the Mind in your back pocket and pull it out anytime
you sense their influence.

THE WORST-CASE SCENARIO: GIVING YOUR-SELF PERMISSION TO FAIL

Once you've talked yourself out of all your other considerations, you may find that there is still one phantom lurking in the gallery of your mind—the fear of failure. It is one of the most pervasive fears in our culture. Yet fear of failure is not inherent in human nature; in fact, failure is a natural part of the learning process. A child learning to walk has no problem with failures. He may fall down a hundred times before he succeeds in taking that first step. It is only as the socialization process begins that children are rewarded for their successes and punished for their failures. They soon learn to conceal their failures from disapproving parents and teachers. Fear of failure is built into our educational system.

Children tend to live up to whatever label they are given. A "fat" child will continue to overeat. A "stupid" child will fulfill the expectation by becoming a slow learner. Parents often unknowingly train their children to become failures and to feel inadequate in whatever they attempt. I lived up to my parents' prophecy that I would fail at anything related to music. For 45 years, my fear of failure stopped me from taking the risk of learning to sing.

People who have an exaggerated fear of failure are overly dependent on others for guidance and decision-making in their lives. Their sense of self-worth is dependent upon other people's approval and they spend considerable effort avoiding disapproval. Letting other people's opinions determine your life is a little like sitting down to an opulent banquet and watching someone else eat your dinner. If this goes on day after day, eventually you die of malnutrition.

People who are afraid of failing cannot handle intimacy and the possible risk of hurt and rejection that intimacy brings. They tend to be cool, aloof and unable to give of themselves. Because of their aloofness, no one feels at ease around them, and their distrust of intimacy brings about the rejection and failure they so desperately fear.

If you want to break out of the cycle that fear of failure creates, you must be willing to court rejection. How many times have you wanted to ask someone out on a date and didn't because you didn't want to hear the word "no"? That word has no power in itself; only your fear gives it power. Rejection can limit your life or drive you forward toward success.

Some of today's most charismatic entertainers suffered rejections and failures that would have defeated almost anyone. An aspiring actor named Sylvester Stallone made the rounds of every agent in New York City looking for work. He was rejected again and again before he finally landed the lead in *Rocky*. After Tina Turner hit stardom, she suffered one defeat after another. Her marriage failed; she lost her money; and for the next eight years she played nothing but cheap clubs and hotel lounges. She couldn't even get an agent to accept her phone calls. Yet she fought her way back to stardom, and her performance is gutsier and more resilient than ever. There are few real successes without some form of rejection as part of the process. These performers succeeded because they were able to withstand rejection and use what they learned to enrich their performances. The painful experiences gave greater depth to their characters and thus to their characterizations. In that sense, even painful experiences are not necessarily *bad*—despite our tendency to label them so. If we can make the leap to labeling each event as just another experience, we can look for the positive aspects. Success or failure is in our own perception. If nothing else, we can view an event as a chance to learn rather than as a failure.

Any time we attempt to break new ground, whether it be in our personal lives or in the larger life of society, we must be willing to risk failure. New ideas are not just swallowed eagerly with the morning's corn flakes—not even in America. Susan B. Anthony lived at a time when women could not receive pay for work, could not wear what they wanted, could not sign contracts or receive inheritances or speak freely in public. For more than 60 years she spoke out against injustice while crowds hissed at her for saying that women were entitled to the same political rights as men. The press ridiculed her. Clergymen denounced her as a dangerous lunatic. Yet she claimed, "Failure is impossible." Her work eventually earned her a place as one of America's great leaders by securing equal voting rights for women.[1]

Successful people do not dwell on failure. They don't attach negative emotions to their mistakes. And they learn to handle rejection. What new ground would you like to break, but haven't had the courage to try? If you truly believed that failure was impossible, what would you do?

People often assume that successful people—life's winners—do things right the first time. But acquiring any new skill is a trial-and-error process. The learning curve does not go straight up. One mistake doesn't mean that you don't have what it takes to succeed. How many times does a toddler fall down in the process of learning to walk? Yet most of us somehow—in our not-yet-adult innocence—kept getting up and trying again. If we can learn to be born again into that willingness to take the risk, we can do anything. And yet, I know people who won't try something new for fear of looking like a beginner. It's their own fear that keeps them from the joy of challenge and achievement.

---

1. Florence Horn Bryan, *Susan B. Anthony: Champion of Women's Rights* (New York: Julian Messner, Inc., 1947), 170.

In judging our own performance, we often use more demanding criteria than we use to measure others' performances. If it doesn't meet our expectations—and it never can—we are likely to view ourselves as failures. The celebrated Czech writer Franz Kafka asked that his novels be burned after his death. At the end of his life, the great Leonardo da Vinci said, "I have offended God and mankind because my work did not reach the quality it should have."

Aspiring to achieve unrealistic levels of success can make us intolerant of our own mistakes. It's a deadly cycle of criticism: The more you criticize yourself, the more incompetent you feel. The more incompetent you feel, the more mistakes you make. The more mistakes you make, the more you criticize yourself.

Stop! Be kind to yourself. Your mistakes are not the issue. The important thing is what you are learning from your mistakes. Furthermore, recent management studies are making it clear that people learn best and change faster when given positive feedback—otherwise known as praise. Figure out what worked, what you did right. Give yourself praise for that part, just as any good manager would. Focus on the positive, and you'll have more energy available for improving the rest.

The late Buckminster Fuller said, "Whatever humans have learned had to be learned as a consequence only of trial and error experience. Humans have learned only through mistakes."[2] These words were spoken by a man

---

2. R. Buckminster Fuller, *An Autobiographical Scenario Monologue* (New York: St. Martin's Press, 1980), 192.

who has been heralded as "the Leonardo da Vinci of our time." Yet at 32 he felt his life was a total failure. He had been expelled twice from Harvard. His first child had died. He was bankrupt, discredited and jobless, with a wife and newborn daughter. As he stood one wintry night on the shores of Lake Michigan, prepared to commit suicide by throwing himself into the freezing waters, he had a sudden realization. He was struck with the thought that his life belonged not to himself, but to the universe; and he chose at that moment to embark on what he called "an experiment to discover what the little, penniless, unknown individual might be able to do effectively on behalf of all humanity." Fifty-four years later he held 47 honorary degrees and 25 patents, and had written 28 books. He circled the globe 57 times, acting as a consultant to corporations and governments throughout the world, proving that his most controversial ideas were practical and workable.

Contemplate this question: What have I learned from the greatest failures in my life?

Part of overcoming our fear of failure is changing our attitude toward adversity. The word catastrophe is defined by Webster's Dictionary as "utter failure." The same word in Chinese means "opportunity." Often opportunity comes disguised as failure. For example, probably one of the most difficult failures to handle is rejection in a relationship. Yet when the pain subsides, you may realize that you were not really happy with the other person. And what would the future be like living with someone who didn't love you and only stayed with you because of feeling sorry for you or not having the courage to leave? Despite the pain, the ending of such a relationship is truly an opportunity for you to discover what you really want in a partnership.

We need to pay close attention to the messages our failures give us. Sometimes people allow themselves to become locked into difficult or defeating situations because they are afraid of being thought of as a quitter. Fear of being seen as a failure can keep people locked into unrewarding jobs or relationships long after it was time to move on. W.C. Fields once said, "If at first you don't succeed, try, try again. Then quit. There's no use being a damn fool about it." Sometimes life requires that we admit that we have failed miserably and have the courage to walk away from a self-defeating situation. My friend Pat, for instance, started out as an oil driller. Now he's a recording artist. He had to find out what he did not want to do in his life before he willingly moved on. I think all of us know someone who got fired from a job and moved on to a better one.

Failures are there to show you what you want to avoid. Experiencing failure can free you to take more risks. Once you have discovered that you can survive a major setback, there is less to lose. The people who are willing to experiment and risk the chance of failure are the world's greatest creators. Most of them have made plenty of mistakes:

- Academy Award-winning director and writer Woody Allen flunked motion picture production at New York University and the City College of

New York. He also failed English at New York University.

- Albert Einstein flunked his college entrance exams and was a poor student in mathematics.
- Liv Ullmann, two-time Academy Award nominee for Best Actress, failed an audition for the state theater school in Norway. The judges said she had no talent.
- Abraham Lincoln failed in business twice, lost 23 out of 26 elections, had a nervous breakdown and lost a vice-presidential race before he was elected President of the United States at age 60.

The truth is that we fail more often than we win. The only people who never fail are those who never compete. People who believe in failure are guaranteed a mediocre existence. Without failure we would stagnate. Most innovations are born of our frustrations and failures. As the late essayist Christopher Morley said, "High heels were invented by a woman who had been kissed on the forehead."

In fact, many mistakes have turned out to be quite profitable products. In the late 1800s the Procter & Gamble Company developed a creamy-white scented soap that it hoped would compete with the popular imported white castiles. A factory worker made the mistake of letting the mixing vat run too long, thereby whipping too much air into the mixture. Instead of throwing away the soap, he poured it into the hardening and cutting frames and the batch was sent out to stores. A few weeks later the company was deluged with requests for the "soap that floats." Bathers no longer lost their soap—it was so light that it popped up to the surface of the water. From then on the company made sure that every batch of soap was given a good long beating. Since that day, more than 30 billion cakes of the floating Ivory Soap have been sold.

The willingness to fail is an important prerequisite to creativity. Certain corporations have begun giving their employees awards for making the most mistakes. They know that mistakes free people to challenge their creativity, and the result will be greater productivity. Creativity and change require decisions, trial-and-error behavior and new ways of reacting to life's challenges. The bigger or more rapid the change, the more we are required to risk. Habit, on the other hand, requires no decisions. We can easily continue our lives on automatic pilot with very little effort. The problem is that many of our habitual life scripts are boring, unsatisfying or even self-destructive. In contemplating a change we need to explore the possible consequences of new behavior and decide whether it's worth the risk. I call this method the Worst Case Scenario:

> Focus on one change that you would like to make in your life that feels risky to you, something that really pushes you beyond your comfort zone. Ask yourself, "What is the worst thing that could happen to me if I took this risk?" Allow yourself to fully feel, visualize and experience this worst-case scenario. Now play with this scene as though you were watching it through an adjustable telescope. Bring it closer to you

so that the scene becomes really large, then shrink it down as though you were viewing it from very far away.

Now ask yourself this question: "Can I accept this possible outcome?" Allow yourself to confront how you would deal with the possibility of failure, rejection or whatever it is that represents the worst possible outcome for you in this new situation.

Finally, consider this question: "What is the worst thing that could happen if I don't take this risk?"

By using this method, you can become more realistic about your risk-taking. By allowing yourself to bring your phantom fears from arm's length into closer scrutiny, you can find out just how real or unreal they are. Then, by distancing yourself from your fears, you learn how to let go of the power you have invested in them. In evaluating the possible outcomes, you may discover that the risk of exploring new territory may actually be more attractive than holding on to an unfulfilling status quo.

THE INNER DRESS REHEARSAL: THE POWER OF VISUALIZATION

Stop. Do not read further. Close your eyes and have someone very slowly read the following paragraphs to you out loud.

Relax and move your awareness to a quiet place within yourself. Imagine that you're in a small Midwestern town in July. It's 95 degrees in the shade and you're walking down Main Street in the heat of the afternoon. The sweat is beginning to trickle down the collar of your shirt. The back of your throat grows scratchy and your lips are dry. You realize how thirsty you are and reach into your pocket for your wallet. Nothing's there. You've forgotten your wallet, and don't have any money to buy a drink. Then you remember that your friend Bud runs a fruit stand around the corner. You turn left at the next block and head straight for Bud's fruit stand.

"Bud," you say, "I'm really thirsty. Can I help myself to some fruit?"

"Sure," he replies. "Take whatever you want."

Some juicy-looking oranges beckon from the fruit bin. You can almost taste the sweetness. You walk over to the oranges and pick one up. You look at the dimpled skin, stick your thumb into it and begin to peel the skin off the orange. As the skin starts to unravel, you feel the citric acid juice squirt onto your thumb. As you pull the peeled orange apart, the juice spurts out into your face. You can hardly wait to bite into it. You look at it and then tear it into sections. You put a section in your mouth and bite into it. The sweet juice pours into your mouth and down your throat. It's the best orange you've ever tasted and you pop the other sections of orange into your mouth, one right after the other.

Right next to the orange bin you notice a basket full of beautiful lemons. You pick one up and admire its bright yellow skin. You take the lemon behind the counter and lay it on a cutting board. Picking up a sharp knife, you slice the lemon in half and admire its perfect symmetry. You pick up a lemon half and squeeze it into your mouth. The tangy juice spurts into your mouth. You throw the remains of the lemon in the trash and chase it down with a glass of water Bud hands to you.

Thanking Bud for the fruit, you head back down Main Street.

Now open your eyes. What did you experience? When people imagine squeezing a lemon into their mouth, many experience an actual puckering of their lips and a contraction at the sensation of sourness. When imagining the sweetness of an orange in intense detail, many people will salivate in anticipation of tasting it.

This demonstrates that thought can create a physiological response. You did not actually have that sour lemon in your mouth, yet your mouth may have responded physiologically as if it were there. In the same way, fearful thoughts can create the sensations of stage fright. With your anxious thoughts, you create the physiological response of adrenaline flowing in your body. Conversely, imagining yourself at ease and performing perfectly can create a physiological relaxation response. Learning the techniques of the inner dress rehearsal—focused relaxation, concentration enhancement, positive self-talk, visualization and inner sensing—can help overcome performance anxiety and make your performance more satisfying and expressive.

The techniques of mental rehearsal have long been used in sports psychology. In sports, as in any performance, there is an unseen playing field where athletes' fears, angers and self-criticisms skirmish in the game of mental control. In my experience as an athletic coach, I found that the proper mental training can turn a benchwarmer into an all-star and make the difference between a losing streak and a chance at the Super Bowl. Since the early 1970s, the techniques of sports psychology have been penetrating the big-time teams. Now some football players practice five-second relaxation drills to release excess tension between downs. Sports psychologist Jim Johnson, working with the Houston Astros, claimed that baseball is only 25 percent physical. "The difference between Triple A ballplayers and big leaguers is mental," he said. Champions throughout the sports world have learned and utilized this secret. Diver Greg Louganis would visualize himself performing the perfect dive before a meet, and figure skater Scott Hamilton mentally rehearsed his famous triple jumps.[1] These athletes have discovered that understanding and utilizing the body-mind partnership is essential to peak sports performance. The same is true for all of life's performances, from stage singing and public speaking to asking for a date.

FOCUSED RELAXATION

The first step in any form of mental rehearsal is focused relaxation. With the mind concentrated and alert and the body relaxed, your physiology will be most receptive to mental impressions and creative visualization. Try this exercise in progressive relaxation. Have someone read the following paragraph to you, slowly, out loud. Or, read this exercise into a tape recorder and play it back to yourself.

> Lie down flat on your back, arms at your side. Close your eyes. Now contract all of the muscles in your face as tightly as you can. . . . Now let go completely of all tension in your face. Let your jaw hang loosely and feel

---

1. Lynn Rosellini, "Horizons," U.S. News & World Report, June 15, 1987,

all your facial muscles unwind and let go. Good. Now tighten the muscles in your neck and shoulders. . . . Now let go and feel all the tension draining from your neck and shoulders. Nice. Tighten the muscles in your arms and hands, clenching your fists, and hold. Now let go and relax your arms and hands completely. Nice. Tighten your diaphragm and stomach muscles and hold. . . . Now let go, letting your chest and stomach sink into the floor, relaxing completely. Now tighten your buttocks and thigh muscles and hold. . . . Now let go, letting all tension in your buttocks and thighs drain from your body, relaxing completely. Nice. Now tighten your legs and feet and hold. . . . Now let all tension drain from your legs and feet, sinking into the floor and relaxing completely. Nice.

Repeat silently: "I am beginning to wind down, to let go of all the tensions in my body. My muscles are relaxing, unwinding, letting go. The tensions are beginning to drain from my body. A gradual heaviness is weighing down my arms, my hands, my legs, my feet, my body. All my muscles are relaxing, unwinding, letting go. Deeper and deeper . . . letting go . . . unwinding . . . and letting go. Noises around me are drifting into the background. I feel the relaxing, the letting go, the unwinding. I am breathing easily and deeply . . . easily and deeply, unwinding and letting go . . . drifting into the peace and serenity of complete relaxation. As my body unwinds and relaxes I enter the peace and stillness, where only these words have meaning. Letting go . . . unwinding . . . letting go . . . unwinding . . . relaxing . . . relaxing . . . let go . . . let go . . . let go . . . I feel peaceful and I relax . . . relax . . . relax . . . relax . . . let go . . . let go . . . let go."

Now lie quietly for a few minutes and then gently open your eyes.

Progressive relaxation exercises such as this one are an important prelude to any other mental training technique. With practice, the body gradually learns to relax completely upon mental suggestion. It is important that you do not fall asleep, but stay mentally alert, letting your conscious awareness move progressively throughout the body. This builds mental concentration at the same time as it relaxes the body. If you have trouble staying awake, I suggest you allow your elbow to remain on the floor while you hold your lower arm and hand up toward the ceiling. Then, if you begin to doze, the arm will relax and fall, awakening you.

This type of effortless, relaxed concentration is the key to a successful, satisfying performance. When you're truly concentrating, it is as though your mind and body are one. In a state of focused relaxation you will find that, without conscious thought, you are doing everything perfectly. There is no internal commentary on your performance. You are simply *being*. You can read about this state of awareness in the book, *Zen in the Art of Archery*.[2] It's called "purposeless tension"—when the archer "ceases to be conscious of himself as the one who is engaged in hitting the bull's eye which confronts him." In a truly electrifying vocal performance, the singer is not self-conscious, but loses himself in the song. The song sings him, as it were, and he *becomes* pure expression.

---

2. Eugene Herrigel, *Zen in the Art of Archery* (New York: Pantheon Books, 1953), 52.

Often this state accompanies a breakthrough in personal risk-taking. After he broke the downhill skiing record, Steve McKinney described his state of mind as "the middle path of stillness within speed, calmness within fear."[3] As you move into unfamiliar situations and begin taking new risks in life, fears and doubts may swirl around you like a hurricane. Practicing focused relaxation can help you find your center in any situation, the eye in your personal storm.

CREATIVE IMAGING

Once you are in a relaxed and receptive state, you are ready to begin working with creative imaging, or visualization. As you may have learned from your experience at Bud's fruit stand, visualization is a powerful technique. As a coach, I used visualization techniques to help athletes develop concentration and coordination. Using imagery helps the body perform correctly by telling it what to do. By visualizing a particular movement, you train the brain to send appropriate neurological messages to the muscles involved. By visualizing successful actions first, you bring to the actual movement feelings of confidence, skill and grace. Neuromuscular training teaches the brain to absorb "perfect" visual images and turn them into skills. Golfer Jack Nicklaus describes his mental rehearsal technique as a film passing before his eyes. "I never hit a shot," he said, "not even in practice, without having a very sharp,

---

3. Keith Thompson, "Concentration," *Esquire*, May 1984: 132.

in-focus picture of it in my head. First I see the ball where I want it to finish. . . . Then, I see the ball going there. . . . The next scene shows me making the kind of swing that will turn the previous images into reality."[4] Arnold Schwarzenegger claims that when he has an image of a particular muscle while doing a pump, the benefit to that muscle is 10 times that of one done when his mind is drifting.[5]

When I began coaching singers instead of athletes, I found that the same techniques applied equally well to singing on stage. By visualizing a flawless stage performance, seeing yourself as you truly wish to be, you can release the star performer within you. Your actual performance will reflect your inner ideal image.

KINESTHETIC AWARENESS

Visualization involves forming a mental picture of how your ideal performance would look. Kinesthetic awareness involves creating an inner portrait of how it would *feel*. Kinesthetic awareness may play as significant a part in the dialogue between the body and the mind as visualization does. Tiny specialized nerve endings embedded in the muscles, tendons and joints, known as proprioceptors, are responsible for reading and reporting on the position of the body and its movements. The ability to read and act on these messages from the proprioceptors is what athletic coaches call kinesthetic awareness. In a study that

4. Judith Zimmer, "Mental Gymnastics," *Health*, August 1984: 52.
5. Keith Thompson, "Concentration," *Esquire*, May 1984: 131.

monitored bodybuilders who were imagining lifting weights, there was a greater measurable muscle action produced when they used a combination of visual and kinetic imagery.

In using the technique of the inner dress rehearsal, I coach performers to imagine how they *feel* during their ideal performance. This brings the kinesthetic dimension to their inner experience and helps to create the partnership between the body, mind *and emotions*.

INNER SENSING

For inner rehearsal of a performance to be most effective, it should actually involve as many different senses as possible—visual, kinetic and auditory. As you allow your creative imagination free reign, you will find your sensory horizons expanding. Sports psychologists are finding that inner sounds may play a part in athletic performances. Golfer Bobby Jones said he often heard a melody on the golf course and that he would play his best game if he used the music to give rhythm to his swing. In fact, some athletes seem to experience direct perceptions of bodily processes. A champion bodybuilder said he heard his muscles growing in his sleep when he was in heavy training; the sound was like "corn flakes being poured into a bowl."[6]

In an inner dress rehearsal for a stage performance, it is important to involve all of your senses, allowing your image to contain as much detail as possible. Try this inner

6. Keith Thompson, "Concentration," *Esquire*, May 1984: 132.

dress rehearsal exercise. Again, you may want to tape the exercise and play it back for yourself. You can use it again and again, especially before you actually have to "perform" at a business meeting or other occasion.

Imagine an upcoming performance. It may be stage singing; it may be a public talk or business meeting. Visualize yourself actually giving this performance in as much detail as possible. See yourself from various angles, as if you were watching a movie. How do you look? What colors are you wearing? How do your clothes feel against your skin? What do your surroundings look like? Feel the atmosphere in the room. Feel your body. Where is your center of gravity? How do your muscles feel? Are they relaxed? See your gestures and body movements. Do they feel contrived or fluid? Notice your breathing. How does your voice sound? Is it loud? Is it soft? What kind of emotion does your voice convey? Are you animated, excited, serious, funny? Look out at the audience. Look into their eyes. How are they responding to you? Are you communicating with them? How do you feel about your audience? Become aware of the subtlest sensation you can feel in your body. Can you feel your fingertips tingling?

Now allow yourself to imagine this experience as perfect; the way you would feel, look and sound during a perfectly satisfying performance. Let the image become stronger, using all your senses. Good. Just be with yourself; feel the satisfaction and fulfillment. Hear the applause of your audience, take in the praise. . . . Breathe deeply and allow the experience to penetrate right into the cells of your body. Feel it fully. Then slowly and gently open your eyes.

I view the imaging process as a continuum. You experience yourself at the beginning, exactly where you are right now. Then you allow yourself to experience where you're going, where you want to be in your peak-performance state. When you create an image like this in your mind, you create a direction. Then everything you do from that point moves you in that direction. I choose to see the process as setting a direction, rather than as setting a goal. Goals can be too static, and we may feel let down once we've achieved them. In truth, we are always in process; we are verbs; we are action; we are ongoing. It is simply a matter of pointing ourselves in the direction we want to go. In that sense, imaging is like setting the rudder on your ship.

In working with imaging, it is important to be patient. Progress in inner sensing cannot be forced. See it as play; be an explorer. Let your imagination run away with you as if you were a child absorbed in a new game. The results may not be as perfect as you imagined, but the performance you give can be closer to your desired results than if you did nothing. You will not be leaving the results entirely to chance. It is true that God helps those who help themselves. So do your part, in faith based on the results of scientific observation, and let the universe do the rest.

FREQUENCY

In any game, life included, there are always obstacles set up to make the game a true challenge. In the inner game of performance, the obstacles are the many varieties of internal interference—doubt, distraction, anger, forgetfulness. One of the main obstacles to a successful public performance is self-doubt. The inner dress rehearsal helps overcome the hurdle of self-doubt by allowing you to prepare yourself internally for the performance. A person performs well if he or she feels confident. We feel most confident when we feel competent, when we know we have done everything we can to prepare. Practice may not make perfect, but it sure makes for a better imperfection.

I once saw Johnny Carson in a live appearance at a charitable event packed with Hollywood luminaries. I was amazed at his cool, calm repartee with the audience, his spontaneous humor and the finesse with which he handled unexpected interruptions in the program. Then I realized, "Of course he's cool, calm and collected. How many thousands upon thousands of times has he done this?" The secret is simple—frequency. If you want to do something well, just do it—again and again and again.

There is really no substitute for adequate preparation, for doing your homework. Sports psychologists who have studied high-risk-takers like Grand Prix race drivers, parachutists and aerobatics pilots discovered that an extraordinary amount of energy goes into preparing for their performances. They analyze every factor that might operate against them and are prepared for any emergency. They are cautious, in the sense of preparing for any possibility, but have learned to take incremental risks. Pushing themselves a bit at a time, they learn to handle new situations and to prepare for the unexpected. Whether engaged in high-risk athletics or stage singing, we have to build up our "muscles" by pushing ourselves to lift more than we can handle if we expect to see any progress. Mental rehearsal gives us an opportunity to flex our inner muscles by visualizing ourselves in risky and unfamiliar situations. It allows us to imagine the obstacles that might arise in a given performance setting and to practice different responses. Imagining yourself going through the motions of a performance prepares you emotionally and physiologically for the performance itself. As you go over it again and again in your mind, your muscles are responding, your nerve synapses are firing, and your positive expectation of a successful performance is being reinforced. This kind of instant pre-play programs your body and mind for success.

OVERCOMING OBSTACLES

As a coach, I taught football players to visualize whole blocks of plays in their minds, trying to visualize every situation that might arise in a game—every defense the opponents might use. The mentally prepared ball player is able to handle contingencies. At any time, he is prepared to change in response to a new play.

When Lee Evans set the world record for the 400-meter dash in the 1968 Olympics, the crowd was astonished. His 43.6-second run set a record. Evans claims that his success involved visualizing every stride of the race, including anticipated emotions that might arise before and during the race, and locating and correcting weaknesses in every step he took. Through rigorous mental rehearsal, he was able to perfect his stride.

In the same way as you would rehearse a race, you can rehearse a performance, allowing yourself to anticipate all the possible distractions and obstacles that might arise. Go over the performance in your mind, moment by moment. Allow your imagination to roam, seeking out possible obstacles or blocks to a successful performance. Let whatever comes into your mind just be there. Someone asks you an intimidating question; a baby starts crying in the back of the room. Notice how you respond. Try out various responses. Do you try to ignore the disturbance? Or do you include it in your conversation with your audience? ("Well, we were all babies once. Remember how that felt?") There is a plethora of responses to any situation. Let yourself play with the possibilities. Through this inner dress rehearsal, you will learn flexibility in your responses to various situations and feel more prepared to deal with whatever arises.

POSITIVE FOCUS

Through inner rehearsals, we begin to see the tremendous power our mental thoughts and images can have on our performance. It becomes more and more essential that we learn to take control of our inner states by weeding out negative thoughts and images and replacing them with positive ones. "When an athlete performs poorly, it's because he allowed an image of failure to enter his mind," claims Ladislav Pataki, Ph.D., a Czechoslovakian sports physiologist. There is no more graphic illustration of this than the story of trapeze artist Karl Wallenda. For years he had performed aerial feats without considering the possibility of falling. Falling was not even part of his mental vocabulary. Then one day, he told his wife that he had started visualizing himself falling. Three months after he started talking about it, he fell to his death. Although some people might call this a premonition, another way to interpret the occurrence is that his images of falling gave his nervous system the message that allowed the tragic fall to happen. By focusing on falling, he created a new path for his brain to follow, and eventually it responded.

The truth that underlies the power of positive thinking is a simple one: "What you focus on, you become." As a sports coach, I trained athletes to inundate their minds with positive thoughts—they were the best, they had what it took to win. I pasted quotes from Vince Lombardi on the locker room wall, such as, "Winning isn't everything, it's the only thing!" In that way, their positive focus was constantly being reinforced visually, as well. The principle can be stated in any number of ways: "Thoughts held in mind produce their own kind," or "What mind can conceive and believe, it can achieve." However you phrase it, the truth beneath remains constant. It is our glory and responsibility to choose.

When working with performers, I use affirmations as a tool to reinforce positive beliefs. Affirmations are positive declarations that help us attain any particular state we may wish to achieve, or change negative behavior patterns or beliefs into positive ones. Affirmations are simply a way of talking to ourselves in a positive manner. The way in which we phrase our self-talk is all-important.

Negative self-talk can affect our physiology as well as our psyche, limiting the freedom of our expression. When you say "I can't," you literally shut down neurological pathways to your brain. Psycholinguistic research shows that a person's mind takes 48 percent longer to understand a negative statement than a positive one.

The secret of using affirmations is to create in your mind the experience you desire in the future, as if it were here now. In truth, any state or quality we may desire exists already within us. It only takes our conscious recognition to bring that quality out of potential and into actuality. To experience the power of positive affirmation, try this eight-step exercise:

1. Think of something you want to achieve—a state of mind, a quality, a new behavior. Remember, your *intention* is the important ingredient.
2. Create a simple sentence that incorporates your desire. The statement should be positive. Use the first-person singular and express your desire in the present tense, as if it were already achieved. An example of this might be: "I am enjoying being more playful."
3. Write the affirmation down.
4. Sit quietly, repeating the affirmation over and over in your mind for several minutes. Let yourself feel the personal meaning the statement has for you as it sinks deeper into your consciousness.
5. Visualize yourself acting and being the affirmation. Hear yourself expressing it. Use all of your senses:

See, feel and hear it in as much detail as you can muster in your creative imagination. In learning to be more playful, for example, you might visualize yourself running through a sunlit field, twirling, letting go and turning somersaults with the playful abandon of a child. Use whatever images evoke the quality of your desired outcome.

6. Boil the affirmation down to one word that expresses its full meaning. The word might be "playful." Use the word as a mantra, repeating it over and over again every time you think of it. Use it for self-talk.

7. Practice this for seven days to allow the message to sink into your physiology and your psyche.

8. Then forget it. Assume that the desired result is complete and a part of your present reality.

All these techniques are designed to help you achieve a sense of personal power and confidence. No producer would ever think of opening a Broadway play without a dress rehearsal. In the same way, the inner dress rehearsal can give you the preparation you need for the "opening nights" of your life's performances. A feeling of being well-rehearsed can be a springboard from which you can be spontaneous and creative during your performance. Your mind is a powerful tool. Use it to perform at your best.

TURNING STAGE FRIGHT INTO STAGE FEVER

Perhaps the earliest known clear example of stage fright is the case of Cicero, the Roman orator. Two thousand years ago, he wrote that he turned pale at the beginning of a speech and would "quake in every limb and in my soul." No doubt, before him there were others, all the way back to some cave woman giving a presentation to her colleagues on the best way to gather grubs. And after Cicero there were such diverse personalities as comedienne Lily Tomlin and dictator Fidel Castro, both of whom have confessed to stage fright.

The fact is that stage fright in itself is not necessarily detrimental. Used properly, it can become the driving force behind an electrifying performance. With training, you can learn to turn stage fright into stage fever.

Most of us, at one time or another, have experienced one or more of the physical symptoms of stage fright: shallow breathing, sweaty palms, dry mouth, pounding heart, goose bumps, shaky knees and a sinking feeling in the stomach. These reactions are part of the "fight or flight" response that was hard-wired into the body's circuitry millions of years ago; it enables us to respond instantly to danger by readying the body for action. That response, which was appropriate in the primeval jungle, is not always as appropriate in a world where "danger" can take the form of a sales presentation, a corporate board meeting or a thousand imagined fears conjured up by our overactive minds. Fighting or fleeing are not very useful responses to such dangers.

The problem is that the body cannot tell the difference between actual threats to its survival or imagined threats. Our internal anxiety about a performance sets the body's defense system in motion, releasing vast amounts of adrenaline and noradrenaline into our system. We are usually doing nothing more strenuous than standing on stage talking or singing. Or we might be simply sitting, talking on a phone and working our way around to asking someone for a date. So the adrenaline is building up tremendous amounts of energy, seeking release or expression. The result is what is commonly called stage fright.

To tell someone who is experiencing stage fright to relax is like trying to tell an inexperienced rider how to rein in a wild horse galloping out of control. It is almost useless. The way to alleviate stage fright is to get the body moving, to release the build-up of adrenaline. Here are a few simple exercises that you can do backstage or in a restroom before a performance to release the tension of stage fright:

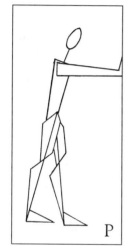

1. Run vigorously in place as fast as you can. To get your voice into the action, sing the syllable "eee . . . eee . . . eee," beginning on a low pitch and rising to a high pitch as you run.

2. Use dynamic tension to get your muscles in action by pushing against a wall as hard as you can (fig. P).

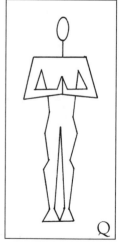

Or stand with your elbows out and raise to chest level, pushing your hands together as tightly as you can. Make an "sss . . . ssss . . . sssss" sound as you push, releasing the breath (fig. Q). Get the air moving throughout the body and allow the breath to follow the movement. In this way, your breathing will normalize.

3. If your knees have a tendency to shake when you are nervous, do some high-stepping, either running

or walking, by lifting your knees as high as you can. Your legs are very powerful and contain the largest muscles in the body. If you can get your legs moving, they will help to mobilize your entire body.

4. To help yourself find a sense of ease and balance in your body, try doing curl-ups: Bend over from the waist toward your toes, allowing your knees to bend slightly, and just hang with your head and arms dangling and your back rounded. You do not need to touch your toes. Slowly begin to stand up by straightening your legs gradually, letting the back of your knees straighten while, beginning in the lower back, you stack each vertebra on top of the other. Allow your head and arms to dangle as you stack. Your neck and head will be the last to stack. Be sure not to lift your shoulders as you straighten your body. Allow your shoulders to hang away from your ears. When you reach a standing position again, rock from your ankles to balance yourself. Take a full breath and exhale.

5. Find your center. Focus your awareness on a point located about four finger-widths below your navel. This is your center of power, the reservoir of life-energy the Sufis called *Kath* and the Chinese called *Chi*. Breathe in and out of this point, feeling your center of power and a sensation of dropping down into your Kath point. This will help alleviate the feeling of butterflies in your stomach and stimulate your inner fire, bringing a feeling of confidence.

These backstage exercises are very effective, but what do you do when you are in a situation where you can't run or exercise when stage fright strikes? Remember what you learned about visualization and the inner dress rehearsal? The body responds physiologically to a thought or visualization. Running in place in your mind can have almost the same effect as physically jogging around the room. If you can't actually do the running, then visualize yourself running vigorously in place; get your body moving in your mind, and remember to breathe. You'll find that your visualization will release the built-up adrenaline. After all, it was your mind that created the fight or flight response to begin with.

Once you understand that stage fright is actually a buildup of tremendous amounts of energy, you can learn to harness that energy to create a powerful force of pure excitement that can captivate an audience. Fear is a two-headed animal. It has the power both to build and to destroy, to energize and to paralyze. Athletes have learned from experience that fear has its advantages. When it smolders instead of burns, it can turn out to be a powerful ally. In their book, *Inner Skiing*, authors W. Timothy Gallwey and Bob Kriegel describe the two faces of fear: "One heightens our perceptions and gives us added energy to perform beyond our normal capacities, whereas the other distorts our perceptions, tending to paralyze us and decrease our competence."[1]

---

1. W. Timothy Gallwey and Bob Kriegel, *Inner Skiing* (New York: Random House, 1977), 56.

Fear can sometimes enable people to stretch them-selves beyond their apparent limitations and perform amazing feats. We all have heard or read accounts of people who developed increased strength when faced with emergencies. A woman with a terrible fear of dogs wrestled a dog pack when she found them attacking her baby. A man backing his car out of the driveway acci-dentally ran over his young son. He single-handedly lifted the car off the ground to free the boy. Like these people who tapped into an unknown source of power when someone they loved was in danger, successful people learn to use their anxiety and fear as fuel to push them past life's hurdles.

The question is not so much whether or not you are afraid, but who is in control—you or your fear. The secret to handling fear is learning to use it so that it serves you rather than stops you. Many people respond to fear with repression or denial. They attempt to push the fear away, to submerge it in their unconscious. Becoming uncon-scious of anything renders you blind and out of control in that area of your life. Repression leads to a feeling of help-lessness—it is the paralyzing face of fear. When you face a challenging situation, don't tell yourself, "I won't be fright-ened." With that kind of an attitude, if you do experience stage fright, you are likely to succumb to it. Instead, tell yourself, "If I do get frightened, I will accept my fear and stay in control." Accept the fear; don't fight it. When you accept your stage fright, in a performance situation, it no longer needs to absorb your entire attention. Instead, you can focus on your performance. Concentrate on the present rather than on what has happened in the past, what may happen in the future or the fact that you are frightened. Let the fear be there, but focus on what you want to express to your audience.

Facing your fears, though difficult, leads to a sense of control, increased self-worth and inner strength. Once you have experienced facing your fears and pushing past your limits, you come out the other side with a new understanding of your personal power.

Fear is not really an enemy. It is a powerful source of energy. Any time you decide to take a new course in your life, you will experience stage fright. In unfamiliar situations you are likely to feel ill at ease, and your anxiety level will rise dramatically at first. If you stay on that course, eventually your anxiety will lessen and the fear will be gone. Let stage fright be your coach, urging you on. Let it talk to you: "Keep going, you're on the right track. Hang in there a little bit longer and you will be finished with this fear forever." Sometimes the best way to get out of your fears is to get into them. Be with your anxieties, allow yourself to experience them fully. In doing so, you will discover new potentials for overcoming these apparent obstacles in your path. Every time you confront the areas you have avoided in your life and tolerate the resulting anxiety, you will find that your fears will lessen. It gets easier and easier.

Don't, however, expect stage fright to disappear overnight. Each time you perform, you unleash your anxiety by expanding your style of personal interaction, and you may experience renewed symptoms of stage fright.

This is actually a good sign. Welcome it as feedback from your unconscious, letting you know that you are blazing a trail through new emotional territory.

Changing stage fright into stage fever is an example of what stress-reduction specialists have termed *thought reframing*. Thought reframing involves changing the context in which we review an experience or situation.

How would you describe what you see in this picture (fig. R)? One person might see a half-empty glass. Another might say the glass was half full. Things have meaning only in the frame or context in which we perceive them. The meaning is whatever we choose to emphasize, and there are multiple meanings to any situation. We tend to frame our experiences based upon how we have perceived them in the past. By challenging these habitual perceptions, we can create more choices in our lives. The key to thought reframing is finding the most useful frame for any experience, so that you can turn it into something that benefits you rather than something that works against you. Thought reframing changes the meaning of your experience.

Every situation, even the greatest adversity, has multiple meanings, as this old Scandinavian folk tale richly illustrates:

While a fisherman and his sons were out at sea, his house caught fire and burned to the ground, destroying all of their possessions in the blaze. When the fisherman returned home, his wife was beside herself with grief.

"We've lost everything," she told him. Her husband, however, took the loss quite calmly.

"A few hours ago," he told her, "a storm came up and we were lost at sea. Then we saw a yellow light that guided us to shore. The fire that destroyed our house was the light that saved our lives."

Folktales from other cultures picture the same wisdom in other words. Viewed in the right context, adversity and change become the fire that kindles new life and greater freedom. We cannot control the external circumstances of life, but we can control our reactions to them. We give ourselves many more options in life by learning to reframe new situations as challenges rather than threats. In dealing with stage fright, we can frame our experience as fear or as excitement. It's the same energy. By changing our perceptions, the sensations we might normally label as *stage fright* can be turned into *stage fever*. This allows us the flexibility to do something new with our performance, to venture beyond the limits of our normal behavior and experience the feverish excitement of a new level of aliveness.

An important adjunct to thought reframing is discovering the *Witness*. The Witness is within each of us. It resides in a changeless and peaceful place inside; it is the Inner Self that remains capable of observing the constant chatter of the mind without becoming identified with its commentary. Discovering the Witness allows us to identify with the part of ourselves that gives us a sense of control and choice because it is not the slave of the mind or external circumstance.

One technique I have used to discover my Witness is to mentally repeat the phrase, "Isn't that interesting." No matter what happens around me, I simply observe, "Isn't that interesting." This technique is very useful in dealing with unexpected occurrences during a performance that might otherwise bring on an attack of stage fright. For example, five people might get up out of the audience and suddenly walk out on your performance. While the mind jumps to the conclusion that they must hate you and your performance is certainly boring, your Witness calmly observes, "Isn't that interesting." In truth, there might be many explanations for the sudden exodus. Maybe they all had a prior engagement. Maybe each had a different reason for leaving that had nothing to do with your performance. Maybe they each needed to visit the bathroom. Maybe the room was stuffy and they needed fresh air. The possible explanations are endless, and none of them warrant you being distracted from your performance. By identifying with your Witness, you can keep right on going, regardless of what distractions might occur around you.

In another situation, you might want to do a reality check with your "audience." Perhaps you are talking to your supervisor about a situation at work, and you notice that she's looking off into space and not listening closely. One response would be to think, "Oh, God, she thinks I'm stupid and I'm boring her." At that point you might feel resentful, flustered or humiliated. But if you call in your Witness to notice her reaction, you might choose to ask, "You seem a little distracted. Is there a better time to talk about this?" For all you know, your boss just found out that her teenage daughter is pregnant, or that the computer ate her most important file. Once again, the audience response may have little or nothing to do with you, but you choose whether or not it becomes a chance to belittle yourself.

One way to short-circuit stage fright is to remember that the objective of your performance is to express rather than to impress. Fear turns the object of our attention inward on ourselves. Excitement turns it outward, toward giving. By reframing your performance in the context of giving of yourself to your audience, you allow yourself the freedom to be in the present, to express whatever is true for you in that moment.

By learning to transform stage fright into stage fever, we experience the exhilaration of taking risks and opening up new options in our lives. The fears that formerly held us back become the feverish energy that lends charisma to all of our life's performances.

A STAR Graduate

At the risk to take command,
When I spoke, when I sang before an audience,
When I shook in my tracks
And my voice quivered tunelessly,
I give credit to myself
That I share the center stage
with no one.

I can see my tiny spore
That had blown on savage thrusts,
Where I'd hope to land would be
Any place but here, And wouldn't you know here is where I hit.

But I liked it.
It feels wonderful!
It is the place I dreamed about
And prayed I would fully find,
That beginning when I first gazed
Into a summer pond
And tears came to my eyes.

For me my hands go wide for all ovation.
I have returned with the fresh and the eager,
Offering me, at last, to me . . .

KENYON, 18 YEARS OLD

CENTER STAGE: THE FINE ART OF RECEIVING PRAISE

Imagine yourself standing alone in the center of a stage. You've just sung the last note of your song. The performance is over. The sound of enthusiastic applause washes over you. One by one, people leap to their feet. The audience, rippling with motion, is giving you a standing ovation.

How do you feel? Embarrassed? Elated? Frightened?

How much praise can you take? How open can you be to receive this acknowledgment?

For most of us, the fear of criticism is an obvious block that stands in the way of performing in public, but the subtler flip side of that coin is the fear of praise. During the early part of the STAR Performance workshop, I ask participants to stand up in front of the room, imagine themselves finishing up a spectacular performance and receiving a standing ovation from the rest of the class. I've witnessed an entire gamut of reactions to this exercise, as well as to actual ovations following the STAR concert performances. Receiving a standing ovation is simply outside the realm of most people's experience, and well beyond their comfort zones. For many people, the experience evokes tears. It's as though a dam has burst within them, releasing the years of fear, self-doubt, criticism and mistrust that have kept them from accepting and receiving heartfelt acknowledgment from others. In a moment of vulnerability the barriers fall away, and a new sense of self-worth begins to dawn. Others experience embarrassment. Many close their eyes, not quite ready to face their audience and accept praise openly. Some laugh, which is a way of discounting the reality of the praise. Still others come away feeling empowered with a new sense of satisfaction in their ability to give and receive in partnership with their audience.

The performer and his audience do not exist in isolation. It is a relationship, a partnership in which both must give and receive in order for a completion to occur and for both to feel fulfilled. This is true of stage singing and theater, as well as all of life's daily performances. In this light, the act of graciously receiving praise can be seen in its true significance. It allows the audience to give to the performer, to participate in the performance and to fulfill its side of the partnership. It creates the circuitry necessary for an electrifying experience for both audience and performer. It allows a flow of energy to occur—a give and take that creates a circle of energy, a wholeness of experience.

However, many of us are not too gracious in our acceptance of praise for life's performances. Let's take a look at some common responses to praise:

Denial

"Sally, you look great tonight. I really love that dress on you."

"Oh, this old thing. . . . I think it makes me look fat."

Rather than receiving the compliment, Sally chose to discount herself and the acknowledgment. The result is that she has in turn insulted the taste and intelligence of her friend.

Passing the Credit

"Jackie, I really appreciate the report you did on the downtown development project. Your attention to detail was fantastic!"

"Oh, it's really Sam who deserves the credit. He did a lot of the research."

Sam may deserve credit, but only after Jackie has gratefully—and gracefully—accepted the compliment made to her. A simple, "Thank you, I'm glad you liked it," would have told the boss that his acknowledgment was important and that Jackie appreciated his interest in her success. Humility is fine, but not if it's used as a mask to hide our insecurities.

Awkwardness and Embarrassment

One of the most common reactions to praise is simply embarrassment—indicated by a blush, a stammered reply or uneasy laughter. All of these reactions are signs that we are not present but locked into conditioned beliefs, self-doubts and fears from our past experiences. The result is that the person who gave the compliment feels awkward. He has caused embarrassment to the recipient of the compliment. The praise was not accepted and the interaction was incomplete.

The best way to get through embarrassment is not to try to hide your reaction, but simply to let yourself be embarrassed and accept the compliment anyway. Admit that you are surprised or taken off guard, and express thanks for the praise given. This defuses the awkwardness of the situation and lets the person know you have received his compliment. In this way there is room for the interaction to continue.

What makes it so difficult for us to receive praise? Almost all children, after going through an initial shy stage, love to be the center of attention. Then, somewhere along the way they get reprimanded for stealing the show and being selfish or self-centered. What parents seldom realize is that children don't reason that abstractly. Every child is the center of his own universe. Perhaps it was that initial reprimand, years of criticism or the idea that praise must be painfully earned, that has led many of us to build resistance to fully receiving the acknowledgment we deserve. We may question the motives of the one praising us, or simply invalidate the compliment. We may let the words in, but block out the love and appreciation that goes with them.

In STAR Performance workshops, I educate participants to notice where they hold back from receiving praise. What parts of their bodies are stiff and unyielding during a situation in which they are receiving? What beliefs keep them from accepting acknowledgment? During the training I ask people to cultivate an attitude of openness, both physically and mentally, by letting their bodies absorb the applause from the audience. I encourage them to look at their audience and acknowledge the reality of their enthusiastic response, and to love themselves more as a result.

Learning to receive praise graciously is an act of self-empowerment, and makes it easier to take the next risk in your life. After a STAR Performance concert, Steve, a graduate, told me that he was so excited about what he had learned that he got up and sang solo later that night at a local club. The audience gave him a round of applause—not just politely, but with genuine enthusiasm. Because of what he had learned during the STAR training, he was able to really receive the applause. That night inspired him to come back to sing, again and again, each time growing more confident. Now he has started his own band and performs regularly in Los Angeles.

As a result of his success in the vocal performance arena, Steve was able to take risks in other parts of his life. Many of his fellow workers were upset because their overtime pay was not being paid in the pay period it was earned. In fact, they often wouldn't see their overtime checks until several months later. Steve decided to gather factual data from his union and take up this case of unfair practice with his boss. He didn't call in the union authorities, but did it himself, with honest feelings. He had no malicious intent. He wanted to be fair and was not demanding, simply sincere. With this kind of approach, his boss had to listen. The boss thanked him for calling the matter to his attention and the situation was rectified. Steve was acknowledged gratefully by all his colleagues for his courage in confronting the situation. Again, he was able to really receive the praise, and let it reinforce his ability to take new risks in his life.

As you take new risks in your life, you will find yourself more and more in center stage. Whether or not you receive a standing ovation from friends and colleagues, it is important to keep acknowledging yourself for your willingness to be vulnerable, and to praise yourself for each successful step along the way to greater freedom and self-empowerment.

EXERCISES

1. Find a quiet place, preferably one where you can be alone for some time as you act out a performance. If you can, actually sing, dance or make your dramatic speech—whatever performance you would most like to do. Then close your eyes and imagine the audience responding with enthusiastic applause. Pick out individuals in the audience and watch them smile and clap. Watch them, one by one, rise in ovation. Imagine it all as clearly as possible. Let

the applause wash over you; let yourself see all those people applauding you. Let all of your feelings come up as the audience salutes you. Open your arms wide to take in more of the sound and sight. Imagine your heart opening up to take in all that emotion. Do this exercise three times a week for a month. Then see if you find it easier to imagine and easier to accept all that praise.

2. Choose a day to compliment yourself all day. Mark it on your calendar and enter it in your appointment book. When you get up and take that first look into the mirror, compliment yourself on what you see. Say something like, "You know, you have really pretty eyes," or, "Gee, your hair looks neat all rumpled like that." Find something nice to say to yourself as you go through the day. "Good for you, for taking the time to eat breakfast today. That shows you are taking care of yourself! I like that color of lipstick; it's very becoming. You were very patient with that driver who cut in on you. I like the way you handled that situation at work; you solved the problem very nicely." The goal is to give yourself a compliment—applause—at least once an hour. You may be surprised at how often you criticize or call yourself names, and how resistant you are to noticing what you do right!

3. At the end of the day, take some time to think back over the day. How did you do? Did you forget to compliment yourself? Did you find it hard to say nice things to yourself? This is another way in

which a journal can help you see your progress. Just noticing what we do and feel can help us prepare to change. For some of us, this exercise will be hard because we've been brought up to believe that it's not *nice* to compliment ourselves. Some of us have been taught that it's downright sinful. We've been taught that we are supposed to be thinking of others instead of ourselves. But one of the great teachers of all time knew better. "Love your neighbor as yourself," He said. Not "more than," not "first." He knew that love of neighbor truly begins with love of self. Those who hate themselves will hate their neighbors, despite what some preachers say. So give yourself—and the others in your world—the best break of all. Say something nice to yourself today.

CHARISMA TRAINING

The audience needs a real person to relate to. The secret of all truly great performers is that they are *present* and *honest* with their audience—what you see is what you get.

No doubt one of the most charismatic performers of all time was Elvis Presley. Once a friend gave me a tape of a 1969 performance in Las Vegas. Elvis began a soulful rendition of "Are You Lonesome Tonight?" and, as happens to many performers, he forgot the lines to the song. He crooned the opening of the song and then his mind went blank.

Without losing a beat, he continued, "Do you gaze at your bonnet and wish you had hair?"

Like any seasoned artist, he knew that if you just fill in the blanks and keep singing on cue, the audience rarely even notices the mistake. But this time the image he evoked was too much for him, and he laughed his way through the next two lines.

By then he was laughing too hard to continue. Meanwhile, the background vocalist kept on singing her lines.

"*You* sing it, baby!" Elvis shouted.

The audience was by now clapping wildly. There was nothing to do but be himself.

"Oh God, oh man, I tell you . . . ," he gasped through the laughter. "The world's a stage and each must play a part."

The background vocalist still hadn't missed a bar. Elvis managed to pull his act together enough to sing the last line.

The audience went wild with applause.

"That's it," Elvis laughed. "Fourteen years right down the drain. Fourteen years just shot right there."

But by the sound of the audience, that was probably one of the most compelling performances of his career.

It takes courage to risk expressing yourself—including your flaws—to an audience, but through that expression you develop the freedom to take greater risks. You will find that the rewards, over time, outweigh both the fear and the times when your risk-taking seems to bring failure.

Honesty is a cumulative process. It begins by becoming aware of what is *present* for you. Keep asking yourself, "What am I feeling right now?" and "What am I thinking right now?" Let it be fine to have whatever thoughts and feeling you have and to take the risk in expressing those thoughts and feelings to others. You may not choose to share each personal revelation with a stranger, but the willingness and liberty to do so is the ultimate freedom.

When your integrity and strength are strong enough that you can be "naked," ultimate freedom exists. The resulting lightness, joy and pleasure is your reward. Those attracted to you will accept your realness and you will not need to pretend. In business, this authenticity will win others to your side and they will want to do business with someone they can trust. People will receive your communication unconsciously because something inside them will ring true when they are with you. When you are real, everyone relaxes in your presence and wants to be near you.

Talent is certainly an important part of performance, as well as doing your homework and study. Rehearsal time and frequency of performing certainly make you more at ease and improve the performance. Being at ease helps create the *real* performance. When you are at ease and can allow your presence to be displayed, that, I believe, is the charisma that is captivating. This ease needs to be available in all areas: body, mind and spirit. Perhaps great talent is really the ability to let go and be what you are, unafraid to display it. Some people do not have the inherent talent but are able to display harmony between body, mind and spirit, expressing totally in their actions and words. It is my contention that this willingness to (as some say) "make an ass of yourself" is what attracts others to you. Perhaps we in the audience respond partly out of a secret wish to be able to "let go" of ourselves in that way. Perhaps we feel more free to be honest, too, in expressing our joy, pain, fear and love. The bottom line is definitely a charismatic performance.

Take Bruce Springsteen. By many standards he would not be considered a trained singer or a great musician, yet he captures the hearts and screams of millions. His performance is spectacular in that he is totally honest with his audience and expresses bodily his feelings, opinions and thoughts. He exposes his inner process and becomes vulnerable. It is this quality that his audiences fall in love with. The words to the song, along with his unique presentation, create a charismatic performance.

Satchmo Armstrong was a fine musician and trumpet player and had a unique vocal sound. His singing performance was not dependent upon vocal quality—it was more dependent upon his style of presentation, sharing his personality with audiences. Audiences fell in love with him.

Think of Sammy Davis Jr., who had talent oozing out of every cell in his body. It was his willingness to display himself and risk not being perfect that allowed his talent to shine. That is probably true with all talented people. What makes the star is the willingness to risk not being perfect and do the work anyway.

Bob Hope is certainly an entertainer with his humor, song and dance. But what is it that makes him a STAR? He would agree that his talent is not necessarily in his dance or song. I believe that it is his willingness to both sing and dance, even though he is not highly talented in those areas. He is himself on stage. He has integrity. He relates to his audience from his heart. His realness, his ease of body and words, his communication create his charisma. He is not pretending or doing an act with his Self—with his material, but not his Self. It is this realness that creates love between himself and his audience. His willingness to "be an ass" gives him power.

In STAR, so many times I am amazed at the quality of voice that appears as people let go of their reservations and hesitations, and just sing. Some have never sung in front of anyone, others have never sung out loud, and then suddenly they are singing with amazingly fine quality, pitch and rhythm. When they combine this with freeing up their body so it, too, can participate with the expression, there are beautiful performances. It is the willingness to take a chance to be themselves in their expression that creates charisma.

Madelyn procrastinated taking STAR for two years. She was frightened and she *knew* she could not sing. She was a secretary, personable but rather shy. She finally took the workshop. What emerged was the beautiful breathy voice of a sexy torch singer. She was surprised and happy with herself. She began vocal lessons and was soon showcasing around Los Angeles. She quit her job and began co-leading workshops on a variety of subjects having to do with body and mind. Her confidence level soared and her whole life changed: it opened and expanded and became full. The release of that torch-quality voice and performance allowed her to express more of her true self and, in the process, created a charisma that attracted others to her. She gained the confidence to reach out and take quantum leaps with her life.

As I look around at the charismatic people in the world, in almost every situation they are people who are willing to take a stand and express what they believe, and whose actions match their words. Even Hitler acted on his beliefs and expressed from his heart. It was his ability to dynamically preach what was real for him, however mistaken and painful, that made others follow and murder for him. Gandhi was the same, in that the power of his heartfelt beliefs spoke through him and convinced others to change the world.

When we express from our hearts and our beliefs, we become powerful, and others listen. When we pretend or are fake, we fall by the wayside. When the body participates freely with our convictions, then there is harmony with our expression, and it makes the presentation all the more charismatic and powerful.

John was shy as he performed in concert. He gave the audience his shyness and did not pretend he was not shy. The shyness came through his song. It was so real, the audience gave him a standing ovation because what they received was him without pretense, and they connected with that core. That is what people fall in love with—not the act. So even though it sometimes feels weird or uncomfortable to tell the truth, that's the risk we really have to take.

In relationships of all kinds—business or personal— others will be attracted to you because of your realness in expression. They will trust you and like you. As your body and mind and attitude become more authentic and congruent, your charisma will be automatic.

I recall Deborah's performance when she stood on stage with tears rolling down her face, talking to the audience about her fear of crying in front of them. She then began her song through the tears. The audience was with her totally. They could identify some small part in themselves and thereby connect with Debbie. The connection is what makes for charisma. When you share your inner process with audiences or individuals, that is what they connect with and are drawn to.

People featured an article about a Japanese boot camp for executives. Among other exercises, participants stood in a shopping mall and sang a song loudly. The reasoning was that the exercise trained the executives to overcome fear of speaking to groups.[1] I suspect it does much more. The ease that is developed will allow them to be more natural in their talks to groups, and a certain charisma will develop that will allow true personality to be expressed. There is great value in risking "being an ass." For one thing, you might find out that you are not as much of one as you always feared!

Perhaps the highest risk in "going public" is that as you practice and change, you may find yourself becoming a powerful person. You may succeed in areas you previously thought forever closed to you. You may very well find this new success and freedom frightening as well as delightful.

1. Michael Neill with David Lustig, "Ever Upward: 13-Day Boot Camp Shows U.S. Executives How to Succeed in Business Through Suffering," *People*, 23 May, 1988: 117-121.

You may find it causes some (temporary) conflict with family and friends who are used to the old, limited (and therefore more controllable) you. It's okay. You can move as quickly or as slowly as you like. You will find strength and courage as you go. You will also find many people to support and applaud you.

Going public with your dreams, however you choose to do it, is what makes life exciting, rewarding and joyous. So I invite you to do it. Find your voice. Sing your own song. Give the people around you a chance to participate in the circle of applause. Let them love you.

ARISTOTLE HAD A NAME FOR IT: THE DYNAMIC UNFOLDING

Entelechy is the dynamic unfolding of who and what we are. Aristotle said entelechy was the realization, the complete expression of a function; it is the state in which a potential becomes actual. It is the blossoming of a flower, the poet writing a poem, the moment when we forget to count and simply dance.[1]

I began my adult life as a science and math teacher. I went on to become a football and baseball coach, a real-estate broker, a businessman, a Rolfer and movement

---

1. Based on the commentary for *entelechy* in the *Oxford English Dictionary*, *2nd ed.* (Oxford: Oxford University Press, 1989) and Jean Houston, "Calling Our Spirits Home," *Noetic Science Review*, no. 32 (Winter 1994): 4.

teacher. Now after serving as a minister in a Unity Church, I am traveling the country lecturing and facilitating workshops, seminars and classes. How did I get from then to now? What was my entelechy?

I lost interest in formal religion during my early teenage years and later became interested in mystical spirituality. I dabbled in various teachings, never pursuing them in depth. As an adult, I wanted to understand human behavior. This led me on a quest for truth through a variety of philosophies, teachings and religious practices, from Judaism to Taoism, from the Tarot to Tibetan meditation. Then I met Dr. Claudio Naranjo, a Chilean-born psychiatrist who was living in this country. He was presenting workshops based on his knowledge of Eastern and Western traditions of spiritual transformation. I spent one week in a workshop with Claudio and was hooked. I wanted more of what this man could transmit.

I began studying with one of his study groups. He became my mentor in the further study of spiritual teachings, from Buddhism to Sufism to Judaism. The experience and teaching that Claudio provided developed my own personal and spiritual transformation.

STAR Performance is the culmination of my own spiritual quest to make Spirit practical and accessible. It is about expressing our inner divinity, the part we refer to when we acknowledge that we are all "children of God." STAR is about uncovering that God-spirit hiding in us; about uncovering the layers that hide our spirit or star quality.

During the years that I have been facilitating STAR Performance, it has gone through quite a metamorphosis.

It is said that necessity is the mother of invention. When I first began facilitating the workshop, it was a three-day training session that culminated in a public concert. But there were increasing demands for a shorter workshop. My wife, Sonya, joined me in facilitating the workshops; together we created a modified version that omitted the public performance while adding new experiences. The new workshop was a one-day experience, and we called it Starshine. To our surprise, the results were similar to those of the weekend format. As our skills and experience grew, we developed a format that made the best use of time and teachings, and participants could have a productive experience in a few hours.

Sonya and I were led to go to Unity School for Religious Studies to prepare for the ministry. Unity is a metaphysical, Christian-based, mystical study that focuses on a positive approach to life. It is based on the Bible and emphasizes the divine essence within each person. While at the School we were employed to conduct a two-hour Starshine program for participants in Unity Village's retreat program. People came from all over the world to attend these retreat programs. We saw our workshop create an experience for these people that in some cases transformed their lives. We learned that these workshops could be tailored to a variety of time frames and still produce exciting results.

My spiritual and vocational paths, my training in different physical and emotional therapies, all led to this point. All that I have gleaned about how we develop our fears and anxieties, as well as how we recover, is incorporated in the workshops. What follows is a simplistic explanation of what I have learned, but it seems to work for many people. I call it the circle map.

THE CIRCLE MAP:
PERSONALITY DEVELOPMENT

We are born stars. We are stars at the center, perfect

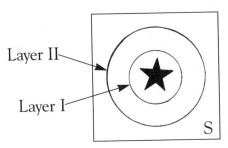

expressions of God, perfect children of God. That *Star*, that *Child*, may also be called the Christ Within or Spirit Indwelling. Some people call it Soul or Buddha-nature. It doesn't matter what you call it. The Star is that part of each person in union with the Divine. As we grow and mature, we develop a layer of conditioning that encapsulates the Star (fig. S).

We are taught all the simple, normal things that are part of learning to live in our culture: "Don't touch yourself that way." "Don't go near the street or in that yard." "Don't open the door when I'm not here." In fact, much of this is necessary for our safety. But many of us interpret scolding as meaning there is something wrong with us, not just with our behavior. We begin to identify with all the negatives that come our way and lose the awareness of our Star. We begin to believe that we are the "bad boy" or "naughty girl," the bundle of mistakes that adults keep pointing out. This is not to say that our parents and teachers don't love us, or that they give us only negative conditioning. It may not be possible to socialize children in any other way. But often children can't differentiate between *making* a mistake and *being* a mistake. And that is when we develop a layer of self-concept that is all the "bad" parts of ourselves. We don't want anyone to see this bad part of who we think we are, so we begin to learn behaviors to hide that first layer. We develop a second layer of armor. This layer consists of various certifications, qualifications and labels that we use to puff up our fragile sense of self. We want to say to the world, "See how great I am. I am a doctor, coach, president, CEO, den mother, tough guy, gold-card carrier, you-name-it. And that makes me All Right."

I have observed that these layers are reflected in the physical body as muscular armor. When someone gets close to us and sees Layer One, we become quite defensive. We don't want anyone to think we are less than or different from Layer Two. Often this is what kills a relationship. People stay together just long enough to see the first layer: all the flowers and candy and perfect romantic dates (sometimes even the first romantic wedding). But the defense can't be up forever, and we know the other person is beginning to see us as we secretly think and fear we really are. Then one or the other cuts and runs, rejecting before being rejected.

The secret is to learn that Layers One and Two may be necessary to help us get along in the world, but they can also become obstacles to the expression of our Star, our spiritual Being. We get through the layers to the Star by accepting the truth that we really are the Star, and then finding or creating experiences that encourage us to express it more and more. That takes risk and courage. Participating in experiences that push through those layers of armor is not comfortable. It may be the hardest work any of us ever does. But the truth is that the Star is our essence. Nothing else really matters.

This is the premise upon which STAR Performance, Starshine and my personal credo have been built. By allowing ourselves to take moderate risks to experience the Star, we go to our next layer of growth. We engage in our entelechy. We can know the Truth and it does indeed set us free.

For many of us, the next phase of knowing and releasing our Star is practicing prayer and meditation. If you are one who is turned off by any religious or spiritual talk, you can stop here. What has been given thus far in the book is enough. But if you want to take a moderate risk, read on.

As a Unity minister, I have learned the value of prayer. I have experienced prayer working in my own life and in the lives of others. But it is not all anecdotal, personal experience that leads me to know the power of prayer. Dr. Larry Dossey reports solid, scientific, controlled-experiment results showing that prayer can influence bacteria in a laboratory dish or the relapse rate of coronary patients.[2] But the studies hold a surprise for us. Some studies have included two prayer strategies: directed and non-directed. In directed prayer, the person praying attaches a specific outcome to the prayer—for physical healing, or for some other

---

2. Larry Dossey, "Healing & Prayer: The Power of Paradox & Mystery," *Noetic Science Review*, no. 28 (Winter 1993): 22.

measurable and desired result. In non-directed prayer, the one praying does not specify the desired outcome. The pray-er simply asks for the best to occur in the particular situation—in other words, "Thy will be done." It is left for God, Christ Essence, the Divine Mind, Love, Higher Power to decide. The studies show that both approaches are effective, but that the non-directed prayer is more powerful. Some researchers suggest that non-directed prayer works better because there is an inherent perfection, wholeness, rightness in the world that manifests itself if all obstructions are removed. If this is true, then we need not tell the universe what to do because God is ready to do what is best for us. We call this Divine Order.[3]

Nevertheless, I don't want to set a formula for prayer. Each of our efforts to interact with God can be unique and honorable. If directed prayer works, then use it in the ways and situations that seem right to you. There will be times when you will be led also to non-directed prayer. Trust your feelings.

These studies bear out what mystics have known and many religions have taught through the ages. In Unity, we teach that prayer is essentially communication with God (by whatever name). So, how do we pray?

To begin, we accept that there is a Divine Presence in the universe. Our task is to align ourselves with that energy, remembering that the true purpose of prayer is to change us or our attitude, not to change God or God's mind. In Unity,

---

3. For more information on scientific exploration of prayer and healing, contact Spindrift, Inc., PO Box 5134, Salem, OR 97304.

we call our directed prayer *affirmative prayer*. Our prayers are not beseeching God to do something for us—not, "Dear God, please get me that new job." Rather, our prayer might be something like, "Dear Spirit Within, I affirm and know that the perfect job for my highest good is unfolding for me now. Thank you." That, of course, leaves the way open for us to recognize new aspects of the current job, or to be directed to a career we had never considered before, or to some other quite unexpected outcome.

So directed prayer might begin with an acknowledgment of Divine Presence, using whatever name you prefer—God, Christ, Spirit, Higher Power. Next, you could acknowledge that you experience and know that the Power is within you. Then express your need or desire in a positive format. You might say, "Spirit within makes me prosperous now," or "The Christ within me is healing this relationship now."

Prayer doesn't have to be complicated or long, nor do we have to resort to the Thees and Thous of King James. It can be very simple—one sentence of plain English. The most important things about prayer are your *intention* and *sincerity*. In a way, this kind of affirmative prayer is like non-directed prayer in that it simply reminds us to work *with* God, rather than demanding that God work *for* us.

But true non-directed prayer goes a bit further. In non-directed prayer, we surrender any and all results completely to the will of God. The 13th-century German mystic Meister Eckhart said, "God is willing to give great things when we are ready . . . to give up everything." And as a prelude to the Lord's Prayer, Jesus tells us, "Your Father knows what you need before you ask Him."[4] Remember, studies show that merely praying "God's will be done" has a greater effect than directed prayer. I am reminded of God's words to Isaiah: "My thoughts are not your thoughts."[5] How can we really know, in the truly grand scheme of things, what is best for us? Shakespeare said it best: "We, ignorant of ourselves, beg often our own harms, which the wise powers deny us for our good."[6] Perhaps that is why, in 12-Step Programs like Alcoholics Anonymous, members learn to pray "only for knowledge of God's will for us, and the power to carry that out."

It's often said that prayer is talking to God, and meditation is listening. The challenge, of course, is that usually God doesn't talk quite as loudly as we think we would like. ". . . the Lord passed by, and a great and strong wind rent the mountains, and broke in pieces the rocks . . . but the Lord was not in the wind; and after the wind an earthquake, but the Lord was not in the earthquake; and after the earthquake a fire, but the Lord was not in the fire; and after the fire a still small voice."[7] If we train our mind to quiet, to let go of some of the chatter, we have an opportunity to hear the still, small voice. There are lots of books about meditation, lots of theories and practices, techniques and teachings. All of them have value in some way, and I encourage you to experiment, to see what works

4. Matt. 6:8.
5. Isa. 55:8.
6. *Antony and Cleopatra* 2.1. 5-7.
7. 1 Kings 19:11-12.

for you. I have learned through my own experience that, like prayer, meditation also can be kept very simple. Once again, intention is everything. It takes time and the discipline of practice to reap the reward.

The effect of meditation is a quiet knowing that we and the universe are in union. There is no separation, only a natural rhythm. Any discomfort or psychic pain usually results from having a sense of separateness from the Divinity that seeks to express through us. To be healed and whole is to experience our connection with this Absolute. Meditation helps us to know this truth, to experience it fully. As we experience our true center, our Star, our Christ within, we become more able to act from that center.

In the Jewish tradition, the famous prayer, "Shema Yisrael Adonay Eloheynu Adonay Echad," is prayed in every synagogue in the world. It is translated as "Hear, O Israel, the Lord our God is One."[8] Hear, O Israel: We are to listen and hear with every fiber of our Being, to quiet the mind and open our perceptions completely to the universal message of God's unity.

We can meditate anywhere, in any body position. Meditation is being mindful of each moment. It is simple, but not necessarily easy. Here are four basic steps: Preparation, Relaxation, Meditation and Thanksgiving.

Preparation relates to the environment. It helps to set aside a place that you use specifically for meditation. That doesn't mean you can't meditate anywhere anytime, but most of us find that if we select and regularly use a specific

---

8. Deut. 6:4.

location, our concentration is enhanced. You might want to set up a small altar with meaningful objects: a candle, pictures or incense—whatever serves to tell you that this is the time and place you exercise your spiritual "muscles."

Relaxation means letting go of tension in the body. Sit comfortably. Then, begin with your feet and bring your awareness up through your body, releasing any tensions you find as you go: feet, ankles, legs, pelvic girdle and genital area, lower back, abdomen, upper back, chest, shoulders, arms, hands, neck, jaw, face, eyes, forehead, ears, scalp. Relax them all, then scan your body once again for any remnants of tension.

This might be a time to practice forgiving anyone that you need to—including yourself. "I forgive the delivery person for knocking over the birdbath," or "I forgive my sister for yelling at me," or "I forgive myself for gossiping about my co-worker, for buying that extravagant meal, for making that mistake."

Now we come to meditation practice. Meditation is going into the silence between thoughts. At the deepest level of concentration, thought may cease and just Being becomes our reality, and we experience the Silence. There are many levels of awareness in the Silence, including what some have called non-awareness, or pure awareness. It is during this time that Divine Mind can speak to us in various ways to suit our needs at the time. It may be an inner-harmonious feeling, an idea, a direct inner knowing, a definite statement or affirmation.

Many of us have been taught to be goal-oriented, to evaluate ourselves according to some criteria learned from others. The experience of meditation is yours and yours alone. Each of us is unique, and it is not helpful to compare ourselves or our experience with what we think someone else is experiencing. We tend to think that everyone else is experiencing God or Bliss or Nirvana or something else that we are not, and therefore that we must be doing it "wrong." But there is no wrong way to meditate, except not to meditate. If we are willing to set the time aside for this sacred experience, to keep the intention of our mind on the single focus, then we have done our part.

Some people find it helpful to use a *mantra*, a word or phrase that is meaningful to them and that is repeated continuously in order to reduce random thoughts. You can say a whole sentence, such as "God and I are one" or "God is my health," or single words like "Peace," "Love," "Christ." Do whatever it takes to create singleness of mind.

Another approach is to use the breath as a guide. Just pay attention to your breathing, observing the in-out, the inhale-exhale. Or just count your breaths. If you lose count, start again. When thoughts come to you, just notice and let them pass like clouds in the sky. Gently return to watching your breathing. Notice what happens in your body, what moves, the temperature of your breath on the inhale and the exhale. In time, your thoughts will fade.

It is a challenge to practice this discipline with no particular goal in mind. However, it is a wonderful adventure. So just sit and narrow your focus to a truth principle or your breath. That's all there is to it. You might want to do this for 10 to 20 minutes in the morning, and perhaps again in the evening.

The last step is giving thanks. When we are ready to stop our meditation, then it is time to be grateful for each breath and for life. Think of all the things you are thankful for: your family, partner, children, friends, situations, shelter, food, body, etc. Gratitude helps our Star shine as we go back out into the world.

Every moment we practice prayer and meditation, we strengthen our conscious contact with God (however it is that we experience and understand that Divine Presence). As that contact is strengthened, we find it easier to rely on that Presence in all our daily business. We find we know how to handle situations that would once have left us puzzled, upset or angry. We find that what we need comes to us just as we need it. We discover that we can do things that once seemed totally impossible, whether it is public speaking or singing or changing jobs or making a commitment to another person. We smile more. We shine.

You are an unfolding, unique, perfect Star. I know that as you practice the ideas presented in this book, you will let your own divine light shine to benefit the world in new and remarkable ways.

FURTHER READING

Aaron, Stephen. *Stage Fright: Its Role in Acting.* Chicago: University of Chicago Press, 1986.

Booth, Leo. *When God Becomes a Drug.* New York: Putnam & Sons, 1992.

Borysenko, Joan. *Fire in the Soul.* New York: Warner Books, 1993.

Brumet, Robert. *Finding Yourself in Transition.* Unity Village, Missouri: Unity Press, 1994.

Butterworth, Eric. *Discover the Power Within You.* New York: Harper & Row, 1968.

Canfield, Jack and Harold Wells. *100 Ways to Enhance Self-Concept in the Classroom.* Englewood Cliffs, New Jersey: Prentice-Hall, 1976.

Canfield Jack and Mark Victor Hansen. *Chicken Soup for the Soul.* Deerfield Beach, Florida: Health Communications, Inc., 1993.

Chagdud, Tulku. *Gates to Buddhist Practice.* Junction City, California: Padma Publishing, 1993.

Collins, Susan. *Our Children Are Watching: Ten Skills for Leading the Next Generations to Success.* Barrytown, New York: Barrytown, Ltd., 1995.

Dossey, Larry. *Healing Words: The Power of Prayer and the Practice of Medicine*. San Francisco: Harper San Francisco, 1993.

Gallwey, W. Timothy and Bob Kriegel. *Inner Skiing*. New York: Random House, 1977.

Harlan, Raymond C. *The Confident Speaker*. Bradenton, Florida McGuinn, McGuire, 1993.

Herrigel, Eugene. *Zen in the Art of Archery*. New York: Pantheon Books, 1953.

Hoffman, Bob. *No One Is to Blame*. Oakland, California: Recycling Books, 1988.

Houston, Jean. *The Possible Human*. Los Angeles: J.P. Tarcher, Inc., 1982.

Johnson, Don. *Bone, Breath & Gesture: Practices of Embodiment*. Berkeley, California: North Atlantic Books, 1995.

Kornfield, Jack. *A Path with Heart*. New York: Doubleday Publishing-Bantam Books, 1993.

Leonard, George. *The Ultimate Athlete*. New York: Viking, 1974.

Merton, Thomas. *Contemplative Prayer*. New York: Doubleday, 1969.

Naranjo, Claudio. *Character and Neurosis*. Nevada City, California: Gateways, 1994.

———. *How to Be Meditation in Spirit and Practice*. Los Angeles: Jeremy Tarcher, 1990.

Ristad, Eloise. *A Soprano on Her Head: Right-side-up Reflections on Life and Other Performances*. Moab, Utah: Real People Press, 1982.

Rolf, Ida P. *Ida Rolf Talks About Rolfing and Physical Reality*. New York: Harper and Row, 1978.

———. *Rolfing: The Integration of Human Structures*. Santa Monica, California: Dennis-Landman, 1977.

Sarnoff, Dorothy. *Never Be Nervous Again*. New York: Crown, 1987.

Shield, Benjamin and Richard Carlson. *For the Love of God: New Writings by Spiritual & Psychological Leaders*. San Rafael, California: New World Library, 1990.

Sinetar, Marsha. *Do What You Love, the Money Will Follow: Discovering Your Right Livelihood*. New York: Paulist Press, 1987.

Smith, Stretton. *4T Prosperity Program*. Carmel, California: 4T Publishing Co., 1991.

Warter, Carlos. *Recovery of the Sacred: Lessons in Soul Awareness*. Deerfield Beach, Florida: Health Communications, Inc., 1994.

Williamson, Gay Lynn and David Williamson. *Transformative Rituals: Celebrations for Personal Growth*. Deerfield Beach, Florida: Health Communications, Inc., 1994.

ABOUT THE AUTHOR

Hal Milton was born in Detroit, Michigan in 1934 and raised by Russian Jewish Orthodox parents. At 13 he moved to Los Angeles, entering a melting pot of immigrants from all religions and nationalities. He quickly assimilated with peers from many cultures and throughout his childhood and adolescence competed in football, baseball, track and golf. During the Korean Conflict, Hal entered the U.S. Navy and played on its football team. Upon discharge he attended college at the University of California at Santa Barbara, participating in intercollegiate athletics and receiving his bachelor of arts degree with honors in physical education. He also earned a master of science in physical education, specializing in physiology of exercise at the University of California, Los Angeles. He then returned to Santa Barbara to become football and baseball coach at a local high school. During his teaching days, Hal continued his graduate studies through the University of Southern California, earning a California credential in educational secondary administration and raising a family of three children.

Then Hal made a major shift in his professional life, venturing into the world of real estate. He soon became interested in broader aspects of the business and opened his own brokerage office. As he began to look at his life in more depth, he sought to know more fully his inner self, and embarked on a spiritual path. Soon Hal shut the doors of his realty business to study with a woman who changed his life—Dr. Ida P. Rolf. With her mentorship, he learned the art and technique of Rolfing and became dedicated to helping people alleviate their pain. He helped them learn how to use their bodies more fully and freely. During his early Rolfing days, Hal continued his studies of other body therapies and movement disciplines such as the Form, Dance Continuum, contact improvisation, Alexander technique, Feldenkrais and Aston-Patterning.®

He was fascinated how, with the aid of these therapies, clients were able to access deep emotional levels and long-forgotten memories. To strengthen his ability to guide clients through various levels of release, Hal began an intensive study of program therapies, including psychological counseling, Gestalt, primal therapy, Neo-Reichian, PsychoSynthesis, BioEnergetics, Rebirthing and Gurdjieff study groups.

His own spiritual progression led him to study with Dr. Claudio Naranjo, who guided him through many psycho-spiritual experiences. Hal became certified as an advisor/teacher in the Pecci-Fisher-Hoffman process of psycho-spiritual integration (the Quadrinity process).

He expanded his specialized practice in Rolfing to

include Rolf movement integration. He continues to lecture and facilitate a variety of workshops, classes and seminars, throughout the United States on methods of evoking charisma while incorporating body, mind and emotions in spiritual awareness.

To expand his consciousness, further his spiritual studies and assist others in doing the same, Hal entered the Ministerial Education Program at Unity School for Religious Studies and became an ordained Unity minister. After four years serving at Unity of Knoxville in East Tennessee, Hal and his wife Sonya, also an ordained Unity minister, are currently traveling the country in support of Inside Out, their alternative ministry devoted to evoking the authentic expression of the divinity inherent in all people.

To contact him for workshops or speaking engagements write:

Hal Milton
c/o Health Communications, Inc.
3201 S.W. 15th Street
Deerfield Beach, FL 33442-8190

HCI's Business Self-Help Books Motivate and Inspire

The Master Motivator
Secrets of Inspiring Leadership
Mark Victor Hansen and Joe Batten

Today's competitive economic climate demands managers who can lead and inspire. Here is the definitive book on motivating others from two of the world's most renowned and respected motivational speakers. Joe Batten—mentor to Ross Perot and author of *Tough-Minded Management*—and Mark Victor Hansen—motivator/communicator extraordinaire and co-author of the bestselling *Chicken Soup for the Soul* series—show you how to achieve top performance from yourself and those you lead: you can become *The Master Motivator*. A must-read for every executive and manager.
Code 3553 . . . . $9.95

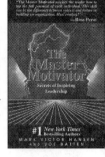

How to Turn Business & Financial Relationships into Fun & Profit
Anne Boe
Author of *Is Your Net-Working?*

Networking Success
How to Turn Business & Financial Relationships into Fun & Profit
Anne Boe

Networking is the business tool of 1990s—a must for keeping the competitive edge that separates the successful from the unsuccessful. Along with networking's unquestioned value in business, it's also useful in personal relationships. Here master networker Anne Boe describes ideas for developing, nurturing and growing your relationships, financial contacts and career networks for peak performance on and off the job.
Code 3650 . . . . $12.95

What You Want, Wants You
How to Get Out of Your Rut
Debra Jones

People in the 1990s are reevaluating their lifestyles as never before. With the stability of tenured positions in large corporations becoming a thing of the past, many workers are rethinking their career choices to be more in tune with what they really want to do. Here Debra Jones, marketing whiz extraordinaire, gives you a game plan for digging yourself out of the quagmire of indecision and hopelessness in order to find your life path. An inspiring book that will leave you revitalized.
Code 3677 . . . . $9.95

The Art of the Fresh Start
How to Make and Keep Your New Year's Resolutions for a Lifetime
Glenna Salsbury

In the #1 *New York Times* bestseller *Chicken Soup for the Soul*, Glenna Salsbury told the inspiring story of her dreams becoming reality. Now she shares her practical, step-by-step approach for tapping into your core being to achieve permanent, repeatable and ongoing self-renewal. This unique approach to goal-setting through internal and spiritual guidance will teach you to live a life filled with hope, joy and a multitude of fresh starts.
Code 3642 . . . . $9.95

Available at your favorite bookstore or call 1-800-441-5569 for Visa or MasterCard orders. Prices do not include shipping and handling. Your response code is HCI.

Share the Magic of Chicken Soup

The #1 *New York Times* bestseller and ABBY award-winning inspirational book *Chicken Soup for the Soul,* along with its sequel, *A 2nd Helping of Chicken Soup for the Soul,* are affordable treasures sure to enrich the lives of everyone around you. Buy them for yourself or as a gift to others. Stock up now for the holidays. Order your copies today.

Chicken Soup for the Soul
Code 262X: Paperback $12.95
Code 2913: Hard cover $24.00

A 2nd Helping of Chicken Soup for the Soul
Code 3316: Paperback $12.95
Code 3324: Hard cover $24.00

Chicken Soup for the Soul Cookbook
101 Stories with Recipes from the Heart

Here authors Jack Canfield and Mark Victor Hansen have teamed up with award-winning cookbook author Diana von Welanetz Wentworth and dished up a delightful collection of stories accompanied by mouthwatering recipes. Seasoned with heartfelt graces, you'll rejoice at the abundance of food and love in your life.

Code 3545: Paperback $16.95
Code 3634: Hard cover $29.95

Available at your favorite bookstore or call 1-800-441-5569 for Visa or MasterCard orders. Prices do not include shipping and handling. Your response code is HCI.